A DECLARATION ON
PEACE

A DECLARATION ON
PEACE

In God's People the World's Renewal Has Begun

Douglas Gwyn
George Hunsinger
Eugene F. Roop
John Howard Yoder

A contribution to ecumenical dialogue
sponsored by
Church of the Brethren
Fellowship of Reconciliation
Mennonite Central Committee
Friends General Conference

HERALD PRESS
Scottdale, Pennsylvania
Waterloo, Ontario

Library of Congress Cataloging-in-Publication Data
A Declaration on peace : in God's people the world's renewal has begun :
a contribution to ecumenical dialogue / by Douglas Gwyn . . . [et al.] ;
sponsored by Church of the Brethren . . . [et al.].
    p. cm.
  Includes bibliographical references.
  ISBN 0-8361-3541-5 (alk. paper)
   1. Peace—Religious aspects—Historic peace churches.
2. War—Religious aspects—Historic peace churches.
3. Pacifism—Religious aspects—Christianity. 4. Historic peace
churches—Doctrines. 5. Fellowship of Reconciliation (U.S.). 6. Just war
doctrine. 7. Interdenominational cooperation. I. Gwyn, Douglas,
1948   . II. Church of the Brethren.
BT736.4.D32 1991
261.8'73—dc20   90-46792
                                                                CIP

The paper used in this publication is recycled and meets the minimum requirements
of American National Standard for Information Sciences—Permanence of Paper for
Printed Library Materials, ANSI Z39.48-1984.

1 2 3 4 5 6 7 8 9 10 96 95 94 93 92 91 90

Contents

Preface

Most Christians and most churches still hold, as they have since the age of Constantine, that war may be morally justified, or even imperative. Therefore they consider national policies of military preparation valid. As we enter the last decade of our century under heightened awareness of the urgent threats we face, we hope for an opportunity to gain fresh consideration of this issue. But we seek dialogue in the context of a renewed vision of the entire purpose of God in the world.

This text is addressed to all Christians everywhere. It also hopes to continue a specific conversation as old as the modern ecumenical movement. One section report from the First Assembly of the World Council of Churches (WCC) at Amsterdam was headed, "War Is Contrary to the Will of God." It stated, "We believe there is a special call to the theologians to consider the theological problems involved" in the diversity of Christian evaluations of war. In response to this challenge, representatives of four groups[1] drafted for submission to the WCC at its Second Assembly, Evanston 1954, a text entitled "Peace Is the Will of God" (see Appendix A).

Already in 1948, just prior to the First Assembly, 78 theologians and church leaders from 15 countries addressed to Commission IV a statement, "The Church—The Christian —and War" (see Appendix B). Its intent was to present to the WCC family of communions a Christian pacifist position on war. Formal conversations have continued ever since.

The state of the question is not very different a third of a century later. Today Christians have become increasingly sensitive to the destructiveness of war. They are consequently more willing to recognize the pragmatic limits on war's viability as an instrument of public policy.

Perhaps not since the Protestant Reformation have so many Christians been so concerned not only about the means and methods of warfare—but also about the social, economic, and spiritual consequences of preparing to wage war. Concerns which have begun to revive the conscience of the churches in a new and discernible way include the following:

The erosion of noncombatant immunity in the modern period.

The indiscriminate character and massive destructiveness of modern weaponry.

The evident trade-offs between military and social expenditures (the former being astronomical, the latter woefully inadequate) at a time of overwhelming hunger, poverty and misery around the globe.

The growing evidence of the irreparable ecological damage wrought by our abuse of energy resources.

The direct attention we hoped would be given ecumenically to the question of the morality of war, as an issue in its own right, has not occurred.[2] Nevertheless, we recognize that many denominations have given considerable attention to the issues of war, militarism, justice, and peace. In recent years the dialogue has included denominations from the World Evangelical Fellowship family of communions in addition to those from the conciliar movement as outlined above.

The three denominational fellowships and the Fellowship of Reconciliation from whose traditions this text speaks ground their witness in their experience of Christ, their Christian practice, and their ongoing theological reflection. For this reason the following statement does not limit itself to the traditional debate around "pacifism," nor does it appeal to the distinctive concepts developed within the separate history of the "historic peace churches."[3] It is stated rather in the terms of a biblical vision common to all Christian communions.

The HPCs and FOR do not claim to be the only Christians aware of how evil war is.[4] They do not claim that their communities' efforts to speak and to serve as instruments of Christ's love are free of pride or ambivalence. Nor do they affirm that their members all wholeheartedly support their traditional testimony.

They note with gratitude a widening tolerance toward conscientious objection on the part of some governments, and growing recognition on the part of fellow Christians that their views have a place in the church. They discern in this recognition a call for a substantial contemporary statement of the grounds for antiwar witness.

Therefore, they write now to emphasize that peacemaking is integral to Christian discipleship. It is the vocation of the church as a whole. So the statement is addressed to the entire church in its fullest sense—all who claim to be Christian.

The text which follows has been prepared on behalf of the four fellowships, under the auspices of their North American agencies. The drafters, convened by John Howard Yoder (Mennonites) consisted also of George Hunsinger (FOR), Douglas Gwyn (Quakers), and Eugene F. Roop (Brethren).

The drafting committee speaks representatively for the four fellowships. They submitted the manuscript to the scrutiny of an international panel. The understanding of the church reflected in the ecclesial institutions of the four fellowships would not permit a statement like this to be juridically "official."

As a witness to the perennial quality of the ecumenical witnessing effort the two earlier FOR/HPC statements mentioned above (Appendices A and B) are included with this new statement. They also attest that many segments of the ethical argument change very little.

The FOR/HPC Consultative Committee

Herman Bontrager (Mennonite Central Committee)
Richard Deats (Fellowship of Reconciliation)
Dean Freiday (Friends General Conference)
H. Lamar Gibble (Church of the Brethren General Board)
William Keeney (Mennonite)
Lauree Hersch Meyer (Church of the Brethren)
Larry Miller (Friends General Conference)
Ben Richmond (Friends United Meeting)

Introduction

Is loyalty to Jesus Christ compatible with participation in war? We believe that it is not.

"Blessed," said Jesus, "are the peacemakers" (Matt. 5:9). What does this mean for us today? We recognize that the challenges of our age invite us to restate the grounds of our stance.

The New Has Come

The world called forth by God, as depicted in Genesis 1—2, is a peaceable world. No antagonism separates the living creatures from one another or from God.

Yet, as the ensuing narratives go on to depict, this peaceable world is soon sundered. The limits established by God are transgressed (Gen. 3). Sibling rivalry degenerates into murder (Gen. 4). Corruption and violence spread throughout the earth (Gen. 6). Relations in the family are tainted with shame (Gen. 9). The futile attempt to live without God in human society reaches, temporarily, new heights (Gen. 11).

So pervasively is the creation disfigured by violence and faithlessness that God is depicted as having second thoughts about its very continuance (Gen. 6:5-13). Finally, through a surprising reversal, a new beginning is made. A single family is chosen as the forebear of a particular nation through whom all the nations of the earth will be blessed (Gen. 12:1-3).

These narratives of primal beginnings signal certain central biblical themes. The peaceable creation—as praised by psalmists, repaired by lawgivers, discerned by sages, and envisioned anew by prophets and apocalyptists—is one way of signifying the goal of all God's ways and works. Whether in acts of rescue and blessing or of judgment and punishment, that goal is never anything less than establishing a creation at peace.

> He will settle disputes among great nations.
> They will hammer their swords into plows
>   and their spears into pruning knives.
> Nations will never again go to war,
>   never prepare for battle again.
> —Isa. 2:4 (TEV)

> I will remove the war chariots from Israel
>   and take the horses from Jerusalem;
>   the bows used in battle will be destroyed.
> Your king will make peace among the nations;
>   he will rule from sea to sea,
>   from the Euphrates River to the ends of the earth.
> —Zech. 9:10 (TEV)

> I saw the holy city, the new Jerusalem, coming down out of heaven from God. . . . Then I heard a loud voice call from the throne, "Look, here God lives among human beings. He will make his home among them; they will be his people, and he will be their God, God with them. He will wipe away all tears from their eyes; there will be no more death, and no more mourning or sadness or pain. The world of the past has gone.
> —Rev. 21:2-4 (NJB)

From Israel to Jesus Christ to the church, according to the biblical witness, God's way to establish peace in the creation has been a history of reversals and surprises. Take the church, that topsy-turvy development in which Gentiles are joined into community with heirs of Sarah and Abraham. This odd community is not only the body of Christ but is given, according to the apostle Paul, an unexpected role to play in peacemaking and reconciliation.

Part of this role is to embody, although often in provisional terms or parables, the initial contours of a new and holy city, the beginning of a peaceable world, as established by God's promises.

> For as many of you as were baptized into Christ have put on Christ. There is neither Jew nor Greek, there is neither slave nor free, there is neither male nor female; for you are all one in Christ Jesus.
> —Gal. 3:27-28 (RSV)

> It is all God's work; he reconciled us to himself through Christ and he gave us the ministry of reconciliation. I mean, God was in Christ reconciling the world to himself, not holding anyone's faults against them, but entrusting to us the message of reconciliation.
> —2 Cor. 5:18-19 (NJB)

The people of God is here depicted as the sign, the foretaste of a world transformed. It is to be a living parable of the new creation—a provisional and communal enactment of the peace offered and promised to all people, all life, and all things. This comunity, incorporated into the very one in whom the old is fulfilled and the new has come, has received a distinctive calling.

It is called forward into the realm of God's *shalom*, in which all will be well. It is called forward from the world sundered by sin and faithlessness into the new and peaceable creation. It is called forward to be by grace what on its own it could not be by nature—a sign, a parable, a witness to the new and momentous thing that has been done in and through Jesus Christ. It is called forward to proclaim and embody the message of reconciliation. In its own common life as well as in its outreach to the world, the community is called to indicate that—by the cross of Jesus Christ—the corruption, oppression, and violence which fill the earth are overcome.

This focus on the people of God does not signal any disrespect for other peoples or other faith traditions. It simply accentuates the *collective vocation* incumbent upon the church and all who adhere to it. Hence, we shall speak here of the people of God as a single subject, recognizing that it may sound jarring to the grammar of individualism and unsettling to the etiquette of relativism.

The people of God is called not to conform to the world, not to reflect the world's painful divisions or its false unities. The people of God is called to be the *transformation of the world*. It is called to manifest healing in the midst of brokenness, love in the face of alienation, and justice in active contradiction to oppression.

Clearly, this transformation cannot be realized merely by a mood of repentance for Christian complicity in war and injustice. Nor is it to be affirmed triumphally as a sublime reality hidden within despairing circumstances. It is to be made flesh through concrete obedience, in fear and trembling.

When men and women unite in this drama of faith, a wholeness appears in this broken present, the original and ultimate wholeness of God's creation, as portrayed in the Bible. When the people of God lives out that primeval blessing and peaceful destiny of the world, it constitutes a powerful sign to all humanity. It becomes a light unto the world, a city set upon a hill (Matt. 5:14).

In this statement we seek to lift up a vision of the people of God, the body of Christ, incarnated in its fullest stature. We are painfully aware how far short our churches often fall from God's uprightness. Yet we point to its concrete realizations in history. And we restate Jesus' invitation to all who would celebrate the mystery of reconciliation, the sacrament of salvation on earth.

As may be learned from the biblical narratives of Israel, Jesus Christ, and the church, the community is to live out its calling in a variety of ways. The unity and diversity of this calling—with special reference to the question of violence—can be brought out, as Christian thought has classically done, by attending to the roles of priest, prophet, ruler, and sage. Although these roles are not fully distinct and in various ways overlap, each may help to clarify the community's vocation of peace.

I
The Priestly Role

Priesthood in Israel

The priestly office in ancient Israel, along with its attendant sanctuary ritual, constituted the means by which harmony was restored, maintained, and celebrated among the people and above all with God. The priests functioned as mediators for the people before God. Although priesthood also included the task of instructing the people in the ways of the law, it was primarily an office of mediation or intercession.

The priest was someone particularly set aside and purified to intercede for the people before the throne of holy majesty in heaven. Intercession took place especially by means of sacrificial offerings, which fell broadly speaking into two main types. First, sacrifices of thanks and praise were offered not only on appointed holy days, but also on the occasion of special deliverances or blessings. Second, sacrifices of expiation, purification, and propitiation—which powerfully dramatized the seriousness of sin and the need for purity in approaching God—likewise occurred both on appointed occasions and at times of special need.

In all cases the sacrificial offerings were costly. The best was reserved for God. In all cases God provided the gift of an animal or cereal to be sacrificed, and God appointed the ritual by which the offering was to be made.

Thanksgiving and expiation may both be regarded, in

this sense, as occurring in a context of grace. Priesthood was thus a gracious institution. It was divinely established to mediate an authentic and unhindered communion of the people with the merciful and righteous God of holy love.

The Priesthood of Jesus Christ

No simple and direct correspondence can be found between priesthood as it existed in Israel and the priestly office of Jesus Christ. In the New Testament priesthood is applied to bring out the significance of Jesus Christ's person and work but the role is profoundly reinterpreted. For the New Testament it is Jesus Christ who interprets the office more than it is the priestly role which interprets Jesus Christ.

Elements comprising the office as it had traditionally been understood are consistently broken down and recast by the New Testament in order to emphasize the point of its deepest concern. The uniqueness, centrality, and mystery of Jesus Christ—especially as they converge in his death for us on the cross—are the core around which all else is interpreted and refashioned.

The New Testament document most attentive to priestly categories—the epistle to the Hebrews—is also the document which subjects them to the profoundest revision. Every line of continuity between the old priesthood and the new is pressed to the breaking point. Points of correspondence are constantly presupposed and affirmed, only to be ruptured at last by the cross.

Priesthood is not exercised without a sanctuary, yet whereas the old sanctuary was earthly, the new is heavenly, not made by human hands (Heb. 9:11). This new, heavenly sanctuary signifies that the ever persistent barrier of sin separating the people from God is removed by the blood of the cross.

Priesthood is not exercised without a human mediator, yet whereas no previous priest was ever free from sin, the new High Priest stands in full solidarity with the people yet without sinning (Heb. 4:15). Sinless mediation by the incomparable divine Son (Heb. 1:1-3), whose death avails for all (Heb. 2:9), is therefore carried out not for himself, but exclusively for the sake of others (Heb. 7:27). The function which no sinful human being as such could discharge, but without which all would be lost, was so fulfilled by the sinless mediator that its repetition is neither necessary nor possible (Heb. 10:18).

Priesthood is not exercised in relation to sin without a sacrificial victim (Heb. 9:22), yet whereas the old priesthood shed the blood of others, the new makes a victim of the priest (Heb. 9:12,14). The old priesthood sacrificed animals; the new priest sacrificed himself. The sanctuary, the mediator, and the sacrifice of the old priesthood all foreshadow the new even though they are finally dissolved by it. By the cross of Christ the office itself is fulfilled and rendered superfluous.

Similar patterns of thought reappear elsewhere in the New Testament. The mystery, uniqueness and centrality of the cross are everywhere repeatedly stressed. No single cluster of concepts and images—whether cultic, financial, military, political, or forensic—can exhaust the richness and complexity of the significance which the New Testament attaches to Christ's death.

It is not necessary, given the purposes of this essay, to resolve the important question of whether the salvation wrought by the cross is meant to free us only from the penalty of sin or from its power as well. The vocation of the church to nonviolence and peace can equally well be established in relation to either view.

Insofar as the cross frees us essentially from the power of sin, the emphasis falls on the work of Christ as a victory.

Insofar as it frees us also from a penalty, emphasis will be laid as well on Christ's work as a vicarious sacrifice.

In each case it is affirmed that something objective takes place—the power is broken, the penalty removed—before the cross can affect us in our existence here and now. Yet in each case the cross is also expected to transform our existence in the present. The power broken objectively must also be broken by the work of Christ in us and among us. The penalty removed, we are also free from all anxious attempts to remove or evade it ourselves by our own efforts.

Throughout the New Testament, the priestly work of Christ's death signifies, first of all, the uniqueness and mystery of divine love. The supreme reason God's love is seen as mysterious and unique is that it spends itself unto death for its enemies. It is not the lovable but the unlovable, not the friendly but the hostile, not the innocent but the guilty, for whom divine love willingly suffers and dies. "Christ died for the ungodly. . . . But God shows his love for us in that while we were yet sinners Christ died for us. . . . While we were enemies we were reconciled to God by the death of his Son" (Rom. 5:5-10, RSV).

The priestly work of Christ's death signifies, furthermore, the uniqueness and mystery of divine righteousness. God's righteousness is seen as mysterious and unique because it remains inexorably hostile toward evil while blessing those who commit it. Human sin is most fully revealed as an outrage to the divine righteousness in the very act by which its consequences are dealt with and removed.

Insofar as Christ is seen as victor, the divine righteousness is established by vanquishing the power of sin. Insofar as Christ may also be seen as vicar, this righteousness is established also by carrying out the verdict against sin in all its severity.

In neither case is any slackening of divine justice seen in the priestly work of Christ's death. In the priestly work of

Christ, God's justice is upheld and established in no other way than as mercy—in the form of suffering love. God's mercy is upheld and established in no other way than as justice—in the form of abolishing sin.

The priestly work of Christ's death, as depicted by the New Testament, is thus something by which our ordinary modes of thought are consistently interrupted. A righteousness in which the guilty are transformed by the suffering of the judge, a love in which enemies are overcome by the submission of love to death—these are as unheard of, it would seem, as is a temple not made by hands, a mediator without sin, and a victim who is also the priest. The cross of Christ as a priestly work cannot be appreciated in New Testament terms unless it arouses a profound sense of rupture and reversal. "For the Son of Man . . . came not to be served but to serve, and to give his life as a ransom for many" (Mark 10:45, RSV).

The Priestly People of God

The New Testament sometimes describes in priestly terms the people who form a community in response to God's call. "But you are a chosen race, a royal priesthood, a holy nation, God's own people" (1 Pet. 2:9, RSV). The priestly vocation of the community is implicitly and explicitly seen to rest on the priestly work of Jesus Christ—"who loves us and has freed us from our sins by his blood and made us a kingdom, priests to his God and Father" (Rev. 1:5-6, RSV; cf. 1 Pet. 2:5).

However, if by the work of Christ the priestly office has been fulfilled by being dissolved and dissolved by being fulfilled, how can the community gathered by Christ be regarded as a "royal priesthood"? In what sense has "priesthood" been ruled out for the community. And in what sense is it still our calling? In what sense does the office continue in the "priesthood of all believers"?

As it centers on the cross, the priestly office of Jesus Christ involves his self-offering to God for our sakes. On the basis of his voluntary suffering on our behalf, the risen Christ offers himself to us as victor and as vicar. As victor he offers himself as the one by whom the power of sin has been broken through his unswerving faithfulness and communion with God under conditions of trial, extremity, and temptation. As vicar he offers himself also as the one by whom the penalty of sin has been borne and removed by the power of divine love in our stead. Either way, his self-offering requires our response.

It is the unanimous witness of the New Testament writings that the community is called to offer itself as wholly and unreservedly as Jesus Christ offered himself to God for all creation. The self-offering of the community in joyful response to God in Christ may be regarded as the heart of the community's own priestly work for the renewal of the creation. The priesthood of all believers is thus a response, a sacrifice of thanks and praise.

A radically new center of loyalty is created for the community which by faith receives Christ's priestly self-offering. What the cross properly inspires is "a sincere and pure devotion to Christ" (2 Cor. 11:3, RSV).

"Worthy is the Lamb who was slain" (Rev. 5:12) is a doxology whose context brings the community's priesthood of response into closest connection with the cross. "Worthy art thou to take the scroll and to open its seals, for thou wast slain and by thy blood didst ransom men [and women] for God . . . and hast made them a kingdom and priests to our God" (Rev. 5:9-10, RSV).

The community's worship is characteristically associated with thanks and praise for the event of the cross. "So Jesus also suffered . . . to sanctify the people through his own blood. . . . Through him then let us continually offer up a sacrifice of praise to God, that is, the fruit of lips that acknowledge his name" (Heb. 13:12, 15, RSV). Thanks and praise cannot be offered by word without also being offered by deed.

The cross certainly means that the members of the community can no longer live for themselves. The community cannot offer itself totally to Jesus Christ—thereby fulfilling its priesthood of thanks and praise—without walking the same way he walked.

It is by walking in the way of the cross that the community actually becomes in the world what it is essentially—"a holy priesthood." In the exercise of its priestly ministry, no part of the community's life may be separated from the whole, nor may the spiritual be divorced from the material. "I appeal to you therefore, [sisters and brothers], by the mercies of God, to present your bodies as a living sacrifice, holy and acceptable to God, which is your spiritual worship" (Rom. 12:1, RSV).

No appeal could make plainer that all aspects of the community's life are to be formed into an integral whole consistent with the way of the cross than this verse: "Do not be conformed to this world but be transformed by the renewal of your mind, that you may prove what is the will of God, what is good and acceptable and perfect (Rom. 12:2, RSV).

How could the community's "spiritual worship" otherwise be defined as a "living sacrifice" that is duly embodied and holy? The community's offering of itself in thanks and praise is to be no less vital, embodied, and holy in its own way than was Jesus Christ's self-offering for us.

Everything in its life without exception is to be assessed by how well and how thoroughly it reflects this responsive and joyful self-committal. Because this royal priesthood has no reason for existence apart from Christ, and because his own priesthood had no other form than that of the cross, the community will not only expect its priesthood to stand in correspondence to his. It will also embrace this correspondence as the highest form of thanks and praise it has to offer him in response.

> For it has been granted to you that for the sake of Christ you should not only believe in him but also suffer for his sake.
>
> —Phil. 1:29, (RSV)

> Blessed are you when people abuse you and persecute you and speak all kinds of calumny against you falsely on my account.
>
> —Matt. 5:11 (NJB)

> When reviled, we bless; when persecuted, we endure; when slandered, we try to conciliate; we have become, and are now, as the refuse of the world, the offscouring of all things.
>
> —1 Cor. 4:12-13, (RSV)

> But rejoice in so far as you share Christ's sufferings, that you may also rejoice and be glad when his glory is revealed. If you are reproached for the name of Christ, you are blessed, because the spirit of glory and of God rests upon you.
>
> —1 Pet. 4:13-14, (RSV)

> But whatever was to my profit I now consider loss for the sake of Christ. What is more, I consider everything a loss compared to the surpassing greatness of knowing Christ Jesus my Lord, for whose sake I have lost all things. I consider them rubbish, that I may . . . know Christ and the power of his resurrection and the fellowship of sharing in his sufferings, becoming like him in his death, and so, somehow, to attain to the resurrection from the dead.
>
> —Phil. 3:7-9, 10-11 (NIV)

Running through all these extraordinary statements is a sense of how completely, how confidently, and how joyfully the community of the royal priesthood is to offer itself to God in Jesus Christ through the Holy Spirit. For the community, no other object of loyalty can take precedence over him. No other object of loyalty is worthy of such devotion and trust. No other object of loyalty can inspire such amazing rejoicing when abuse, dishonor, and loss are suffered for his sake.

It is not surprising, therefore, to read, "But I say to you that hear, 'Love your enemies, do good to those who hate you, bless those who curse you, pray for those who abuse you.' " (Luke 6:27-28, RSV). Is not a community which strives to embody these practices and attitudes simply expressing its loyalty to the one who laid down his life for us all? It would be surprising, however, if this community were to believe that any other objects of loyalty somehow could be so momentous that its commitment to Jesus' way of the cross would have to be significantly modified, qualified, or restricted.

Such claims, which of course have dominated the life and teaching of the church at least since Constantine, will need to be examined more fully at a later point.[5] Yet it is clear here what direction our essay must take. Can it really be that neighbor-love, for example, represents such an overriding interest for the believing community that the community would at times have no choice but to resort to violence against a distant neighbor, called "enemy," for the sake of protecting a near neighbor? Is violence for such a purpose really the proper way for believers to relate to the tragedies of history?

We cannot affirm that loyalty to the nation-state (whichever one it might be) would be such that the church would be called to put aside or circumscribe its commitment to the way of the cross. We deny that the body of Christ must lend its members to the enterprise of defending and preparing to defend the nation-state against its real or merely putative enemies by means of organized military force and violence. Could it credibly be said of such a community that it consists of those who would prefer to die rather than to deny their faith in Jesus Christ?

II
The Prophetic People

Prophecy in Israel

The role of the prophet in the biblical tradition cannot be confined in a single definition. As singer, messenger, lawyer, seer, or poet, the prophet was the instrument of encounter between the people and their God. The prophetic oracles declared that God saw the misery caused by economic exploitation. God heard the cries of those abused by political power. God knew the confusion created by distorted religious practice. God was acting to save. The God of Moses and Miriam, Joshua and Deborah, was not a passive onlooker. This God was a powerful presence acting in the midst of both the people of God and the world.

The prophets often used the "day of Yahweh" (a term probably drawn from the military vocabulary) to portray the power of God. This "coming day" was to be a moment of judgment and mourning for those in Israel or elsewhere who anticipated a future that would continue their own prosperity at the expense of others (Amos 8:4-10; Joel 2:28—3:21, RSV). "God's day" would right a world characterized by paralyzing oppression and escalating violence.

Occasionally the prophets point to a coming one. This figure was to be an "anointed" instrument of divine intervention, marking the inbreaking of God's new world. The roots of this messianic expectation lie in Israel's experience of monarchy.

Christians were not the first to misuse the prophetic

voice and vocabulary, although it is easy to document how the churches have appealed to the divine warrior image to justify various kinds of violence in God's name.[6] The power carried by the prophetic word in the ancient world brought with it the danger that national, economic, or social groups would attempt to exploit it. They might use that power for their specific programs or interests, rather than allow it the freedom to announce God's *shalom*.

Ancient Israel struggled to discern the true from the false prophet in their midst (Jer. 23:9-22; Deut. 18:21-22). For example, an unnamed prophet anointed Jehu king of Israel, prompting one of the most bloody revolutions in the history of ancient Israel (2 Kings 9:4-10).

But the warrior figure was not the only image used by the prophets to announce God's powerful presence. They used many metaphors including spirit, road builder, farmer, carpenter, physician, judge, lover and shepherd (Amos 9; Hos. 14; Mic. 7; Isa. 11, 40; Ezek. 37).

The prophetic understanding of God as warrior is rooted in the liberating act of God in the exodus. Because *God* is warrior, Moses—the archetypal prophet—instructs the people that it is not up to them to fight: "And Moses said to the people, 'Fear not, stand firm, and see the salvation of the Lord, which he will work for you today. . . . The Lord will fight for you, and you have only to be still' " (Exod. 14:13-14, RSV).

The work of a prophetic people is to announce the active presence of the Holy One. This is a precarious calling. The future toward which the Holy One acts cannot be predicated on the present or on any single vision of the future.

Nevertheless, the prophetic tradition displays a consistent vocabulary of human relationships that characterize God's coming world. In Hebrew, in addition to peace (*shalom*), that vocabulary includes such words as justice (*mishpat*), righteousness (*sedeqah*), steadfast love (*hesed*), and compassion (*racham*).

Each of these has its own distinctive meaning. Together they describe social structures marked by integrity and mutuality. These structures work on behalf of all people, including those marginalized by physical misfortune or social circumstances.

Jesus as Prophet

First-century Jews expected an eschatological prophet to come at the end of time. Both Jesus and his predecessor John were seen in light of that hope. Jesus in Luke 11 spoke of the fate of many past prophets as if he were expecting to be one of their number. In the fourth Gospel and the early testimonies in Acts, Jesus was seen as the "Prophet" fulfilling in a final way the promise of Deuteronomy 18:15ff.—according to which God would raise up a prophet "like Moses."

By his very existence, Jesus is God's prophet. Thus he announces that the prophecy of God's justice is fulfilled in our hearing (Luke 4:17-21). Jesus identifies this with those prophets who extended the love of God beyond the boundaries of the nation. In consequence, Jesus suffers persecution. He is the prophet who suffers rejection from his own (Luke 4:24-29).

Clearly the New Testament uses *prophet* to describe Jesus' actual social role as proclaimer of God's righteousness. Whenever Jesus is spoken of as revealing the Father, or whenever his presence and his words condemn injustice, this too is seen as prophecy.

The Prophetic People of God

Prophecy is one of the gifts exercised in the early church. Moses desired that all Jahweh's people should be prophets (Num. 11:29). Joel predicted, "Your sons and daughters shall prophesy" (3:1, NJB and 2:28, RSV). Both Moses' desire and Joel's prediction are initially fulfilled when the Holy Spirit is poured out at Pentecost.

Sometimes prophet is described as the specific role of a few particular individuals (Acts 21:9ff.; 1 Cor. 12:29). Elsewhere it appears as a kind of speech to which any believer may be inspired (1 Cor. 11:5). It encourages, improves, and consoles (14:3).

Like Jesus the people of God also prophesies by its very existence. By the fact of being a "chosen race, a holy nation," it declares "the praises of him who called [them] . . . into his wonderful light" (1 Pet. 2:9, NIV). In addition, this *prophecy* "teaches the ruling powers" of this world what has been God's plan through the ages (Eph. 3:9-10, NIV). Jews and Gentiles are to be united in one body. That proclamation not only reveals history's direction under God. It also invites and empowers every hearer to be drawn into that victory.

This prophetic word is "spoken" by the very fact that Jew and Gentile, slave and free, enemy and friend, belong together in one body (Gal. 3:28; Col. 3:11).

It is spoken as well by words announcing God's righteous intentions and denouncing injustice. It is spoken by actions of creativity, by deeds and words of solidarity with the oppressed, by the struggle to transform social structures in consonance with God's justice and mercy. These struggles inevitably place the church in conflict with the prevailing social and economic structures, and with the "natural rulers" of the land.

Even as Jesus was often in the company of the Zealots, political prophecy will place God's people in the midst of political pragmatists and violent situations. Christians will constantly face temptations to yield to pragmatic grounds for violent responses to conflict, rather than seeking nonviolent alternatives. This is why Paul clarified, "For though we walk in the flesh, we do not war according to the flesh, for the weapons of our warfare are not of the flesh, but divinely powerful for the destruction of fortresses" (2 Cor. 10:3-4, [NASB]).

The temptation to political violence must necessarily return us to the challenge of the cross. It calls us back to the prophetic perspective of the crucified one. If we attempt to move beyond the cross we reduce it to nothing more than the instrument of our forensic acquittal. It becomes a pardon for those who accept the offer, leaving us free to deal with evil and conflict using the same instrumental pragmatism the world employs.

We are then tempted to compromise truth with what appears to be common sense, to temper obedience with expedience. The prophet's knowledge of God's righteous purposes would thus be appealed to as justification for the force of political deception, for violent revolution, or for repressing political opposition.

It was pragmatism that caused Caiaphas to conclude that "it is expedient for you that one man should die for the people, and that the whole nation should not perish" (John 11:50, RSV). Caiaphas spoke truth in a way he never dreamed. But our vocation is not to be right in the way Caiaphas was right. When we make expedient choices for violence as the lesser evil, we force God to work out our salvation in spite of us, rather than through us.

Certainly, God can make even the worst violent human actions serve divine purposes in history. Isaiah (Chapter 10) pointed to Assyria as God's instrument to chastise Israel. The Isaiah of the Exile pointed to Cyrus as God's instrument for releasing the Jewish people from Babylon (Isa. 44:24—45:7). Paul (Rom. 13:3ff.) and Peter (1 Pet. 2:13ff.) affirmed that the pagan rulers (who were to persecute both of them) had a role in God's peacemaking purposes. Caesar did not need to be Christian for his role to be under God's control.

Nevertheless, any good end that political and military actions of pagans may unconsciously serve is a matter separate from the role of a people consciously dedicated to knowing and doing God's will. The people of God must be a coherent sign from God to the world. They must be a conscious attempt to realize the encounter between God and humanity.

To resort to the violence of instrumental pragmatism is to deny the power of God as revealed in Jesus. It amounts to crucifying Christ anew to save ourselves. This holds the grace of God up to contempt (Heb. 6:6). When the church does this, humanity can only conclude that nothing is new in Christ. The gospel is one more self-serving ideology among others. The church is merely another sociological reflection of the world. A violent church is a blasphemous sign indicating that the people of God has lost its authenticity.

When we stand resolutely at the cross, we stand at the turn of the ages. We see that the inbreaking reign of God is not predicated upon the visible possibilities of the present. We are loath to take up the cross ourselves, to share in Christ's cup of radical obedience. But is the servant greater than the master (John 15:20, RSV)? At the cross we abide in the power of the risen one who faced temptation before us and overcame. Thus our nonviolence, our faithfulness in Christ, substantiates human hope and gives evidence of things not seen (Heb. 11:1). It constitutes the most powerful sign the prophetic people of God can perform in a war-wracked world.

III
The Discerning People

Wisdom in Israel

Wisdom is a third stream in the biblical tradition. The sage in ancient Israel was the educated, literate, wise figure of the community. Wisdom was an international phenomenon. Ancient Israel shared proverbs, riddles, and didactic stories with its neighbors. The sages were not only recognized as wise in their own community; they often functioned as international diplomats and messengers. They knew that moral discernment existed beyond Israel's borders. They understood that the bonding of insight extended beyond the confines of a single group, whether political or religious.

The theological roots of Israel's wisdom tradition lie in its *interpretation of God's ordering of the world*. God sustains a predictable world—one in which vegetation yields seed of its own kind (Gen. 1:12). God sustains a just world in which the integrity of the upright guides them to life, while the evil of the treacherous destroys them (Prov. 11:3,5-6,19; 12:28, etc.). God sustains a peaceful world in which a dry crust of bread, eaten in peace, is better than a house full of feasting torn by strife (Prov. 17:1).

In wisdom's perspective, violence is foolishness, whether it be the violence of the tongue, the arm, or the social structure (Prov. 20:17; 21:6-7; 22:8). In God's world, acts and consequences cohere. Therefore, if one sows evil and violence, one should expect to reap evil and violence.

This cause-and-effect connectedness does not depend on human agency but on divine direction. Therefore, the sage can observe that it is better not to repay evil, but to wait upon God's help (Prov. 19:11; 20:22).

Like the services of the priests and prophets, the discernment of the sages could be influenced by their role in the society, by a particular political situation, or by traditional understandings that did not remain open to new light. Thus the discernment of Eliphaz, Bildad, and Zophar helped Job only to the extent that they goaded him toward a perception of God's world different from theirs. Those sages who did not remain open to the future would be rendered irrelevant when a new action by God called into question previous discernment.

> Therefore I will yet again shock this people, adding shock to shock:
> the wisdom of their wise men shall vanish
> and the discernment of the discerning shall be lost.
> —Isa. 29:14 (NEB)

Jesus as Wisdom and Word

Little in the heritage of wisdom could have prepared the sages for God's new action in Jesus Christ. The Gospel accounts report that the discernment by Jesus astounded even the most learned (Luke 2:46-47). In his own teaching Jesus used the language and literature of the ancient sages—but in new ways.

The parable, a special tool for education and entertainment in wisdom circles, became, according to the Gospel writers, one of Jesus' favorite teaching forms. The parables of Jesus continue to capture the attention of listeners, urging them toward a world where enemies are treated as neighbors and all are invited together to the feast.

Those apocalyptic blessings we know as the Beatitudes point also to the relationship between acts and consequences. Blessed are the peacemakers; for they shall be called the children of God (Matt. 5:9). By articulating the Beatitudes in a wisdom genre, in an apocalyptic setting, the community has preserved them not as dreams about a heavenly tomorrow, but as discernment about a very real today.

It is not only when Jesus teaches in proverb and parable that he represents wisdom. The fourth Gospel begins by confessing that in him the "Word" (*logos*; analogous to the *hochma* [wisdom] of Proverbs 8) had taken on "flesh" (*sarx*). As person, in his full human particularity (Jewish, not rich, not violent . . .) Jesus not only *speaks* but *is* divine wisdom. It is only as such that he empowers others also to become God's children, partakers in God's nature and therefore instruments of God's continuing work.

Like the fourth Gospel, the letters to the Hebrews (chap. 2) and to the Colossians (1:24—2:8) affirm a clash between the faithfulness incarnate in Jesus Christ and other notions of wisdom. These are the passages in the New Testament where statements of the divine dignity of Christ are the strongest. But in each text, the humanness of Jesus, and his suffering, are the keys to the claim of wisdom.

Wisdom in the People of God

The strongest statement about the gospel of the cross as wisdom is that of Paul (1 Cor. 1:18—3:3, 3:18—4:3). Here is revealed an awful wisdom that confounds the wisdom of the world.

The doctrine of the cross is sheer folly to those on their way to ruin, but to us who are on the way to salvation it is the

> power of God. . . . Divine folly is wiser than the wisdom of
> man, and divine weakness stronger than man's strength.
> —1 Cor. 1:18, 25 (NEB)

Paul fully avows the dissonance between the cross and this-worldly notions of wisdom and power. He utterly refuses to grant that his witness is other than the way things really must be. He calls his readers not merely to know about this wisdom as a kind of private information, but to incorporate it as the law of their life.

For the church, as for Jesus, wisdom is opposed to the way our culture sees power working. Beyond this, the discerning people of God partakes, as did sages of old, of an international, cross-cultural consciousness. While faithful to the uniqueness of the Christian revelation, they also acknowledge points of contact with other value systems.

They not only teach, they learn from Gandhi in India, from Buddhists in Vietnam, from secular social sciences in the West. They observe that religions and philosophies converge in some dimensions of their witness to God, to righteousness, and to reconciliation. They know that the hope of God's kingdom is not confined by national, cultural, or even religious boundaries. They realize that notions of holy wars and crusades against so-called "infidels" blaspheme against the universal love and freedom of God, who constantly interjects divine activity into the midst of human life—whether correctly discerned or not.

Thus, the discernment of God's people extends beyond the boundaries of its own faith tradition. It calls Christians to serve as diplomats, interpreters, and messengers across religious and cultural lines of defense. It calls them to be allied in joint ventures for justice and peace on earth. This outward movement in the world is inseparable from the inward movement toward God and from the truth value of the cross, in which the mystery deepens with every step. Every explicit witness to the truth of God in Jesus must there-

fore be offered out of a deep respect both for the un-
fathomable paradoxes of God and for the countless diver-
sities of human experience.

The people of God partakes of the transformation of the
world, witnessing to the *oneness* of the world that already
exists and that is still being created by the one God. It resists the foolishness that would set law against law, culture
against culture, one part of the whole against another. To
love one's enemy is the touchstone of our witness to the ultimate transcendence and intimate immanence of our Creator and Redeemer. It may have to be a witness borne in
the face of extreme alienation and brutality.

But to mirror the aggressor's hostility would be to yield to
the god of this world, the father of lies, the murderer from
the beginning. Thus to yield is to let the world transform
the people of God. This is the epic tragedy that predomi-
nates in Christian history.

Using the rhetorical genre of ancient wisdom, James re-
minds us of the unity of cause and effect, of means and
ends.

> Can a fig tree . . . yield olives, or a grapevine figs? No more
> can salt water yield fresh. . . . And the harvest of righteous-
> ness is sown in peace by those who make peace. What causes
> wars, and what causes fightings among you? Is it not your
> passions that are at war in your members? You desire and do
> not have; so you kill. And you covet and cannot obtain; so
> you fight and wage war.
>
> —James 3:12, 18—4:2 (RSV)

The discerning people of God lives by the pentecostal
power of the Spirit which Christ has poured out on all
flesh. Because the risen one, who is the future of all creation, is present in the Spirit, the church knows the unity of
ends and means and the ultimate unity of all things. Because the Spirit is poured out on all flesh, the people of

God can appeal to the divine wisdom which is deep within all peoples.

The outcome of true justice is inseparable from ways of peace. Outward wars are the fruit of conflict within hearts that are not at peace in the one God.

The person who confesses Christ and yet goes to war is not yet a faithful witness to the world's unity under God's grace. These are hard words. Jesus wisely counsels us to pray that we not be led into temptation but delivered from evil. But if we wage war, whether in self-righteous vengeance or in avowedly regretful pragmatism, we pit justice against mercy as concretely as we pit "our side" against "the enemy."

Christ calls us to *participate* in saving grace, not simply to appropriate it for ourselves. Jesus' death for the godless fails in us if we do not allow it to extend through us to others. The disciple must be willing to be the last victim in the cycle of violence, thereby breaking the cycle. The life-giving Spirit of the risen one is inseparable from the self-offering Spirit of the crucified one.

The discerning people of God therefore participates in the great drama of life and death. Amid the warring and competing forces of the world, this people is given the privilege

> to enlighten all men on the mysterious design which for ages was hidden in God, the Creator of all. Now, therefore, through the church, God's manifold wisdom is made known to the principalities and powers.
> —Eph. 3:9-10 (NAB)

This multifaceted reconciling wisdom unfolds in faithfulness to Christ. It unfolds in the experience of weakness, poverty, and vulnerability which overturns the logic of power and its imperatives. Yet the wisdom of God is by no means naive to the ways of wealth and power. Christian peacemakers will be found in the corridors of power waging peace through lobbying, peace education, and mediation.

The peace witness will sometimes find us before the powerful not only as advocates but as defendants: "and you will be dragged before governors and kings for my sake, to bear testimony before them and the Gentiles" (Matt. 10:18, RSV). Peace witness may include acts of nonviolent civil disobedience such as placing our bodies in the path of the instruments of war or boycotting systems of institutionalized violence. Thus, Jesus sends us out "as sheep in the midst of wolves; so be wise as serpents and innocent as doves" (Matt. 10:16, RSV).

The reconciling of principalities and powers does not start at the top of the power structures and trickle down from there. In the wisdom of the cross, it begins at the base, among the powerless, the oppressed, the vulnerable. Wisdom is not ratified at the summit. Instead, "wisdom [*sophia*] is justified by all her children" (Luke 7:35, RSV). Thus, sophia (*hochma*) invites all to learn together from her (Prov. 8—9). But her pupils will be gathered especially from those less tempted by the prerogatives of power.

In the discerning people, God is engaged in the *restoration of all things* to their rightful place in creation. This takes place as the various races and women and men regain their intended relationship of equality and mutuality with one another. The dismantling of racist and patriarchal norms and structures subverts one of the traditional foundations of militarism in history.

But this restoration must also extend to the earth itself, in a renewed sensitivity to the harmonies and rhythms of God's creation. As James had said, human strife is rooted in an alienated lust for more of the earth's bounty. As we have killed and pillaged one another for control and enjoyment of natural resources, we have also depleted the earth and interrupted life-sustaining cycles, threatening life on earth.

The ecological crisis is not merely a misperception about the balance of nature. It is failure to discern God's oneness. To restore our sense of the earth's integrity and limits is no less crucial than to restore our sense of human unity in the oneness of God. Hence monotheism, a living faith in one God, Creator of a coherent heaven and earth, is not simply a first tenet but the ultimate historical mission of God's people.

IV
The Royal Servant People

Monarchy in Israel

No institution gained more visibility in the history and tradition of ancient Israel than the royal office. David represents the epitome of that office in the tradition, if not also in the history. Even after kingship in Israel ceased to be a political reality, the community longed for and expected one like David, in the line of David, to take up the royal scepter.

Economically, the coronation of David both followed and fostered the movement from primarily subsistence village farming and herding to a more diversified and centralized national economy. Socially, the royal government both followed and prompted a move from decentralized leadership by the village elders to leadership from centralized segments of society such as the priests, the merchants, and the military.

In spite of the central role played by the king in history and theology, ancient Israel never fully embraced the royal ideal in its standard ancient Near Eastern form. At the time of Samuel, Saul, and David, some groups apparently rejected the change in social patterns and theological understandings required to make room for a king. These groups, represented in the biblical tradition by Samuel, insisted that God never intended the people to be ruled by a king (e.g., Judges 9; 1 Sam. 8).

Later groups, while not necessarily objecting to the existence of royal leadership, condemned the actual deeds of particular kings of Israel and Judah. These critics, found frequently but not exclusively among Israel's prophets, pointed to the unfaithfulness and incompetence of the king as the cause of the sin, distortion, and suffering obvious throughout the community. Their denunciation of royal unfaithfulness ranged from Ahab's worship of Baal (1 Kings 18), to Ahaz' reluctance to await Yahweh's rescue of Jerusalem (Isa. 7), and to Zedediah's refusal to surrender to the Babylonians (Jer. 27:12ff.).

Nevertheless, the king became integrated in many streams of the biblical tradition. He was seen not as an unwelcome interloper in faith and history, but as a son of God, designated to lead the people.

> I will tell of the decree of the Lord: He said to me, "You are my son, today I have begotten you. . . ."
> —Ps. 2:7, (RSV)

Regardless of the activities of some of Israel's kings, Israel retained the hope that the king would effect deliverance for the people and maintain a just and prosperous society.

> He [the king] will judge your people in righteousness,
>   your afflicted ones with justice.
> The mountains will bring prosperity to the people,
>   the hills the fruit of righteousness.
> He will defend the afflicted among the people
>   and save the children of the needy;
> He will crush the oppressor.
> —Ps. 72:2-4 (NIV)

With each coronation the people anticipated that the newly anointed king would be not a problematic despot but God's faithful son and servant (Isa. 9). They restated the ideal that his rule would contrast with the royal mode of other nations (wives—alliances, horses—military technology, gold) because of his familiarity with God's law (Deut. 17:16ff.).

Once monarchy in Jerusalem had been abandoned, and Israel's calling was to live among the nations, future hope was sometimes expressed in the language of kingship. The messianic expectation anticipates a royal figure who will be entrusted with maintaining *mishpat* and *sedeqah* (justice and righteousness) on behalf of the poor and needy, sometimes through military power (Ps. 72).

As the messianic expectation moved through the prophetic tradition, new dimensions arose. For example, some prophets declared that the Messiah's activity would benefit people to the ends of the earth as well as the chosen few (Isa. 11). Others relativized royalty by saying that it would be from the temple rather than the throne that justice would go out to the nations (Mic. 4; Isa. 2).

In the biblical narrative, poetry, and liturgy, the king was designated not only God's anointed (*messiah*) and son (*ben*), but also as servant (*'ebed*). The biblical tradition joins royal and servant language in Nathan's announcement to David.

> Go and tell my servant David, "Thus says the Lord. . . . When your days are fulfilled and you lie down with your fathers, I will raise up your son after you, who shall come forth from your body, and I will establish his kingdom."
> —2 Sam. 7:5, 12 (RSV)

One can scarcely overstate the influence of this prophecy as it was passed on and adapted from generation to generation. Reinforced liturgically in the Psalms (e.g., 89), this announcement not only legitimized the Davidic monarchy in ancient Israel. It also preserved the later Jewish messianic expectation through the Persian, Hellenistic, and Roman periods.

While this designation of the anointed (*messiah*) as God's servant now seems natural in the Christian tradition, that very familiarity can hide a serious problem. Calling the king "servant" can provide one more symbol to legitimize concentrating power in the hands of designated leadership.

That seems to have been a problem already in ancient Israel. In the prayer that follows Nathan's oracle, David deferentially and repeatedly refers to himself as God's servant (2 Sam. 7:18-29). But in the prayer that very repetition could serve to reinforce the claim of the Davidic dynasty to a unique position of power over others not chosen servant. And so the prayer ends,

> You, Sovereign Lord, have promised this, and your blessing will rest on my descendants forever.
> —2 Sam. 7:29b (TEV)

Even today, the use of the servant language by those in power often camouflages the royal will-to-power.

Jesus as Royal Servant

By appropriating the title, "Son of David," the early Christians declared Jesus heir to that royal office. The prophets of the exile further extended the messianic portrait by announcing that the royal Messiah suffers, even dies, as the act of salvation by the holy one of Israel (Isa. 52—53). The reign of God announced by the prophets comes through one who gives up his life rather than bringing about a new world by a military campaign.

Jesus repeatedly rejected sovereignty won by force (John 6:15; 18:36). This reality required the early Christians to transform the Messianic understanding of the royal tradition into the form in which it is found in 1 Peter.

> When he was insulted, he did not answer back with an insult; when he suffered, he did not threaten, but placed his hopes in God, the righteous Judge. Christ himself carried our sins in his body to the cross, so that we might die to sin and live for righteousness. It is by his wounds that you have been healed.
>
> —1 Peter 2:23-24 (TEV)

Here was a royal servant who would come to power and exercise power not by military might but by a love willing to suffer even unto death.

The Royal Servant People

Jesus said to his disciples,

> You know that among the gentiles those they call their rulers lord it over them, and their great men make their authority felt. Among you this is not to happen. No; anyone who wants to become great among you must be your servant.
> —Mark 10:42-43 (NJB)

Can the community that carries on Jesus' suffering servant model of royalty employ authoritarian structures to effect change simply because the world is so structured?

Since the time of the Emperor Constantine, the churches have been tempted to wield official power or political clout whenever available. Christian history is littered with failures to resist the temptation of royal domination masked as "servanthood" at the institutional level.

Yet one also finds a great "cloud of witnesses" (Heb. 12:1, RSV) from the underside of Christian history. They are those who, through chosen or circumstantial weakness, have served as earthen vessels, bearing treasures of service, hope, and love to a suffering humanity (2 Cor. 4). The hiddenness of this other history only confirms that in our culture (churches included) we still are tempted to read history as the struggle, particularly through wars, of the powers.

The royal servant people of God celebrates the ascent of Christ to the throne of God as the revelation of Christ's final and decisive authority in heaven and on earth. Yet with John the church also affirms that this ascent began as Jesus was lifted up on the cross of suffering and death. On earth, Christ's power and authority are witnessed and exercised in the world through our conformity to his death.

The royal servant people understand from the Gospels that the royal identity of Jesus remained ambiguous on earth. This is epitomized by his crown of thorns and his enthronement upon the cross (John 19). While his glorification in heaven is absolute, his presence on earth by the Spirit remains subject to the ambiguities which characterized his ministry in the flesh. This included respecting human freedom in all, both high and low, friend and adversary.

In preaching and in living, in mission and service, the royal servant people must be faithful to this vulnerable dynamism. For the kingdom to come "on earth as it is in heaven," the rule of Christ must be exercised in a non-coercive decentralized form. This form is relative and thus relevant to human conditions of history, culture, and politics.

Divine power is effected by the workings of truth in human hearts. Those who confess Christ have found their defenses overwhelmed by the victorious truth of the risen one. Hence, the faithful know that Christ's truth has no use for human tactics of self-defense, whether personal, communal, or national, at the expense of the life or dignity of others.

The royal people thus follows Christ in his vocation to "bear witness to the truth" in the face of power (John 18:37). At the same time, they realize that power will often treat truth as irrelevant and expendable (v. 38), paying mock tribute with a crown of thorns (19:2).

The outcome of Jesus' earthly ministry must not be taken as a failed attempt to seize power from Rome. From the outset of his ministry to Gethsemane, Jesus repeatedly faced and rejected the temptation to claim power and authority for himself. He saw each possible power path—economic, religious, and political—as demonic. As he rejected them, he found divine power undergirding him (Matt. 4:1-11).

The people of God participates in a royalty that "is not of this world" (John 18:36, RSV). *Nevertheless*, as the body of Christ, this people makes Christ's truth concrete in this world. This people is by no means apolitical, acceding to any policy. It is not an ideological organ for political power, sanctifying oppression and violence. The royal servant people is politically engaged and partisan, working with and for movements that embody more just and equitable economic relations, more peaceful resolutions to conflict, and the broader distribution of authority and decision-making in society.

Yet the reign of God is not coterminous with or the same as any given culture, government, or political movement. The people of God allies itself with specific political powers only insofar as those powers are moving in the same direction as God's reign. Such alliances cannot therefore be principled or official. They are merely operative in specific events and activities—and constantly open to reappraisal. God's intent is the inbreaking of a *shalom* far more inclusive than merely taking sides in the world as it is.

The royal servant people will resist temptations to the righteous crusade or holy war, whether defending democracy from the right or just revolution from the left. The church's sharing in God's favoring of the oppressed and exploited cannot partake of violence against the oppressor. That tactic finds no precedent in Jesus. It can at best achieve a trading of places between oppressor and oppressed, aggressor and victim.

Following the Prince of Peace, the church remains subject—that is, answerable and in dialogue—to civil power (Rom. 13:1). In this role, Christians will continually plead the case of peace and justice through whatever avenues the political process allows—and sometimes through actions the authorities forbid. Solidarity with the victims of civil power may lead to acts of open disobedience to civil authority.

The royalty of Jesus before Pilate consisted in his vocation to "bear witness to the truth" (John 18:37). That vocation continues in the royal people as it attempts to speak truth to power, letting the power of truth work in the human heart despite awareness that power will often treat truth as moot (John 18:38).

Such awareness should serve not to inspire resort to coercive power but to renew commitment to stand with the powerless and exploited people at the broad base of society. It is there that abusive power has wounded so many. And it is there that the truth often burns bright in human hearts, uniting them in love and cooperation.

In a similar vein, the church will at times implement the very rights the government itself fails to administer. Such civil initiatives can include providing sanctuary for refugees and resisting the development of the arms of mass destruction, appealing to the provisions of international law. In such initiatives, the people of God asserts its reality as a transnational and cross-cultural power for peace and human rights.

The invitation to Christ's messianic banquet is open to all. The Christian cannot curtail that invitation by refusing to accept all, by supporting capital punishment of criminals, or through violent retribution against the corrupt.

Still, as in Jesus' loving call to the rich young ruler (Mark 10:17-22) and elsewhere in the Gospels, the invitation addressed to the elite tilts toward the claims of the poor. Sharing of wealth, broadening participation in policy-making, simplifying lifestyles in modesty—these are the seeds of peace. Failing to sow these, any people will perennially reap war.

The reign of God on earth, a joyful order of just peace in interpersonal relationships and social structures, comes mysteriously and surprisingly, as Jesus taught repeatedly in his parables. The insignificant-looking mustard seed becomes an impressive tree and a support to life (Luke 13:18f.).

And as the teller of parables himself became the parable, that truth became even more resonant. "What is sown is perishable, what is raised is imperishable. It is sown in dishonor, it is raised in glory. It is sown in weakness, it is raised in power" (1 Cor. 15:42-43, RSV). The call of Jesus comes to us across the ages: "Increase our faith! . . . If you had faith as a grain of mustard seed. . . ." (Luke 17:5-6, RSV).

V
Conclusion

The biblical revelation witnesses to a wholeness in creation that, though presently fragmented, is caught up in a vast process of restoration. God is working out that healing through an infinitely subtle array of instruments. God's people, one social locus of reconciliation on earth, is an important instrument. As the sign of divine *shalom*, God's harmonious and just peace, God's people lives out a challenging, often dangerous mission to a divided and hostile world.

We have noted that four facets of that peoplehood are found in the history and teachings of Hebrew Scripture. God's people is called to be priestly, prophetic, wise, and to serve. The New Testament witnesses that these four facets are embodied, fulfilled, and universalized in the life, death, resurrection, and ascension of Jesus Christ—and in the pouring out of the Spirit on all flesh.

The church as the body of the Risen Christ—alive, breathing, and moving by the power of the Holy Spirit—shows forth the reality of God's salvation on earth through its own enactment of the same four facets of life as God's people. Participation in war at the behest of the nation state, even for good causes, denies each of them. This is the case not merely on the basis of rigorous moral standards but because of the very nature and mission of the church. Following Christ is the way of the cross. The mystery of human redemption is being worked out in our very bodies. When the people of God embodies the peace of Christ *now*, it becomes a sacrament of salvation for the world.

The way of peace is no easier for us to follow than it was for Jesus. We pray to be spared his agonizing ordeal. Yet we know that the blood of his covenant reaches beyond us, and that we may be called to complete in our bodies what is lacking in Christ's afflictions (Col. 1:24), that God's gift may flow on to others.

We root our hope in Jesus, who ended his words to his disciples thus: "I have told you these things, so that in me you may have peace. In this world you will have trouble. But take heart! I have overcome the world" (John 16:33, NIV).

APPENDIX A

Peace Is the Will of God

by
Historic Peace Churches and International
Fellowship of Reconciliation Committee,
Geneva, Switzerland, October 1953.

Editor's Note:

In October 1949 W. A. Visser 't Hooft, general secretary of the WCC, invited the peace churches and the IFOR to produce statements on the Christian basis of pacifism. The Continuation Committee of Historic Peace Churches and IFOR, established in May 1949 in Europe, responded in July 1951 with "War Is Contrary to the Will of God," a document which contained separate statements from the four groups plus a joint introduction.

When the publication "War Is Contrary to the Will of God"—the title of which picked up the assertion of the Amsterdam Assembly of the World Council of Churches—was presented to the staff of the World Council of Churches, there was mixed reaction. On the one hand, ecumenical leaders expressed appreciation to the peace churches and the IFOR for following the appeal of the assembly to direct theological attention to the problem.

On the other hand, regret was expressed that the publication was not a unified statement. If the peace churches themselves, it was said, could not unite on a position, how could they reasonably expect a council as diverse in denominational and political backgrounds as the WCC to arrive at a common mind?

The continuation committee, therefore, addressed itself to this task. At a meeting held in The Netherlands in September 1952, it was agreed: "This conference recognizes that the challenge [to produce a unified statement] of the World Council of Churches is an opportunity which should not be lost and . . . reaffirms the decision . . . that we attempt to prepare such a statement."

With heavy drafting involvement by younger Mennonite scholars and British Friends, the continuation committee was able to produce an agreed-upon statement within one year's time. This was published as a response to the "special call" of the Amsterdam Assembly for theological attention to war/peace issues. It was presented with this attitude:

> We do not profess to have a detailed solution to the international problems of today's world, but we believe that our conviction confirmed by several centuries' experience of the full pacifist position deserves more thorough consideration than has yet been accorded to it.

It concluded with the "hope and in the conviction that the perplexity acknowledged by the Amsterdam report must not remain the church's only answer to the world's great need. . . ." It was also published in German and French translation.

It should be noted that usages which now sound dated, including sexist terminology, have been retained for the sake of historical accuracy.[7]

I. The Common Christian Faith

The World Council of Churches was constituted on the confession that the "Lord Jesus Christ is God and Saviour." The Christian men and women who met in Amsterdam, representing millions of Christians from every corner of the earth, were deeply conscious of man's failure and despair apart from God and of the serious crises of our own time. But they had met to proclaim that "there is a word of God for our world. It is that the world is in the hands of the living God, Whose will for it is wholly good; that in Christ Jesus, His incarnate Word, Who lived and died and rose from the dead, God has broken the power of evil once for all, and opened for everyone the gate into freedom and joy in the Holy Spirit; that the final judgment on all human history and on every human deed is the judgment of the merciful Christ; and that the end of history will be the triumph of His Kingdom, where alone we shall understand how much God has loved the world" (10-A).[8]

The Council's proclamation that "War Is Contrary to the Will of God" thus rested on a clear conviction of the supremacy and finality of Christ. It sensed the incompatability of war with his "teaching and example." Eleven years earlier the Conference on Church, Community, and State at Oxford had expressed the same conviction thus: "The universal church . . . must pronounce a condemnation of war unqualified and unrestricted. War can only occur as a fruit and manifestation of sin" (59-Ox). This Conference, under deep realization of the transcendence of the Christian community over earthly social divisions, had urged that our starting point in consideration of war be "the universal fellowship of Christians, the Una Sancta." And at another point it had pleaded: "The first duty of the church, and its greatest service to the world, is that it be in very deed the church—confessing the true faith, committed to the fulfillment of the will of Christ, its only Lord, and united in him in a fellowship of love and service" (57-Ox).

Whatever may be our judgment as to particular credal statements, we are in agreement with the consensus of Christian faith as expressed at Oxford and Amsterdam. It is on this basis that we for our part have come to reject war. Since "war is contrary to the Will of God" it would seem to be incumbent on every Christian to abstain from it. We are convinced that the unreadiness of most Christians to come to this practical conclusion reflects the thinking quite general within Christendom, in which alongside of Scripture certain pseudo-Christian or secular attitudes and assumptions have gradually and at times unconsciously been accorded axiomatic status. A number of these will be briefly examined here.

II. Some Extraneous Presuppositions Influencing Christian Thought

a. The inviolability of natural social bonds

While there can be no doubt of the essential unity of mankind, a man's personal experience of community is limited to the very small number of individuals with whom he can share life. World society is therefore built up by social groupings of infinite variety in kind and size. This structure, however distorted it may become at times, is rooted in the order of creation, as is seen in the divine establishment of the conjugal tie and the family which grows up around it. Yet this is the very structure whose distortions are an immediate cause of war, for from time immemorial the needs and desires as well as the pride of one social group have come into conflict with those of another. In these conflicts each group has a self-consciousness which is expressed by the instinctive sense of loyalty which each member of the group feels. Perhaps nothing has ever seemed more detestable socially than that a member of a community in time of common danger should flee or should betray the common cause. Indeed, the right and duty of group self-defense is considered axiomatic in every society.

The problem then arises whether Christ accepted this group solidarity as an axiom, consequently implying that his new ethic was to be practiced within the limits of natural community, leaving its absolute claims inviolate, or whether the ethic of the clan was to be supplanted as ultimate norm by that of the Christian brotherhood. Is *agape* intended in the final analysis to transcend all other impulses of social cohesion? In other words, can the Christian at the moment when his nation is faced by military attack from without refuse his social responsibility to fight in its defense on the grounds that Jesus said, "Love your enemies"?

At first thought the answer to this question seems obvious. Christ confirmed the created order of society; he strengthened, for example, the marriage relationship and lifted it to an even more inviolate level. Some would conclude that the tendency among Christians to accept the claims of the natural community, including military service, as axiomatic and as absolute can therefore be justified.

On the other hand, however, we encounter in various settings the "dark" sayings of Christ, in which he seems openly to contradict his general attitude. "You must not think that I have come to bring peace to the earth; I have not come to bring peace, but a sword. I have come to set a man against his father, a daughter against her mother, a son's wife against her mother-in-law; and a man will find his enemies under his own roof. No man is worthy of me who cares more for father or mother than for me. . . ." (Matt. 10:34-37, NEB). " 'Who is my mother? Who are my brothers?' And stretching out his hand toward his disciples, he said, "Here are my mother and my brothers. Anyone who does the will of my Father in heaven is my brother and sister, and mother" (Matt. 12:48-50, NJB). To this might be added his own attitude at the moment of supreme danger, when Peter, "moved by the natural instinct of group loyalty and the ethic of the natural community," drew his sword in defense, only to hear from his Master, "Put your sword back, for all who draw the sword will die by the sword" (Matt. 26:52, NJB). In all this we learn that Christ consciously subordinated the imperfect ethic of the natural community to the perfect ethic of the Christian brotherhood, although he fully realized the inevitable hostility that arises within the natural community when one of its members subordinates his group loyalties to the transcendent ethos, the *agape* of the Christian community. We therefore believe that Christian participation in war can be justified neither by the natural instinct of loyalty nor by the ethical norms of the natural community. It is impossible for the Christian to prefer citizenship before discipleship or to argue that any part of his relations with his neighbor should be based otherwise than on obedience to his Lord.

To us it seems clear, then, that in the light of the gospel of Christ neither the right nor the duty of the defense of self or of others at the cost of the life of an "enemy" will stand examination. Furthermore we do not believe that those values of liberty and cultural heritage which are often unconsciously identified with Christianity and cited to justify wars of "defense," can be defended by war. War, even when conducted against an aggressor or an occupying power, inevitably involves the destruction not only of human life and of instruments of civilization but also of the very moral and spiritual values which it seeks to defend. But even if a particular war were likely to preserve more lives and values than it would destroy (leaving aside the impossibility of such calculation) it could never be the duty of a follower of Christ to take the lives of some of God's children in the hope of protecting the lives and liberties of others.

The interpretation of solidarity, according to which the church's or the Christian's ethical duty is identification with a particular class or with the interests of a particular nation, is in truth a contradiction of the distinctively Christian solidarity with all of mankind, demonstrated by Jesus when he answered the question, "Who is my neighbor?" with a parable about a Samaritan, thus showing a startling disrespect for Jewish national sentiment. Christian love is distinguished from customary human behavior precisely in this, that it overreaches the bounds which natural group solidarity sets to unselfishness. The distinctively Christian ethical teaching is not that we should love our neighbor, but that every man is the neighbor whom we must love. "If you love those who love you, what credit can you expect? Even sinners love those who love them" (Luke 6:32, NJB).

b. The medieval Christian concept of society

In the great but mistaken medieval vision of the *corpus christianum* the kings of the earth were thought to have been brought into the Kingdom of Christ, the natural and religious communities being regarded as coterminous, synthesized in the universal empire and the universal church. Though that *corpus* has largely disintegrated, its social and political ethos still persists today. Influenced in part by subconscious medieval attitudes, the church is unwilling to break with the political and even economic status quo of the social order within which she finds herself, maintaining the delusion that in some fashion she is salvaging that order or discharging her responsibility for it by this very dilution of her own substance. We are grateful that the Oxford conference called attention to this problem in the following words: "The church had not yet faced the new situation with sufficient frankness. With the conservative instincts of all institutions of long standing and influence, it has fought a defensive—and on the whole a losing—battle for the maintenance of as much as possible of the old ideal of the *corpus christianum* and of the privileges and authority which that implies" (200-Ox).

The persistence of this medieval attitude is seen also in

the church's readiness to support the military operations of the nation in which she finds herself, identifying the cause of the fatherland with the cause of God. Another vestige of this tradition is the survival of the concept of the divine right of kings in the form of the readiness of Christians to take up arms in obedience to the state, to which they have transferred the absolute authority once erroneously attributed to the monarch.

c. The concept of the "just war"

Within the medieval tradition was developed the Augustinian-Thomistic concept of the *just war*, a concept resting on the premises of the *theologia naturalis*. Whatever our attitude toward natural theology as such, the concept of the just war represents a construct of human reasoning which is at variance with revealed truth. Furthermore, it disregards the distinction to which we shall refer later between the dispensation of preservation (or providence) and that of grace (or redemption). It is reasoned that since the state is responsible for the common weal and since the war in question is fought in its defense, such war is just—just not only politically speaking, but also in the sense that its execution is not sin. In other words we have here a suspension of the divine absolute law and will. Whether and under what circumstances Paul in Romans 13 would permit a state to engage in war in execution of its responsibility to maintain order is an open question; that such action could ever be just in the sense of involving no guilt is untenable.

It is of no mean importance that the validity of the just war concept for our time is being challenged, even by the tradition most closely bound to Thomas Aquinas. In *Institutiones Iuris Publici Ecclesiastici*, a recent Vatican publication, appears the following remarkable assertion: "Today a just war which would permit a state to attack in the interest of obtaining its right no longer exists" (translation ours), though under certain conditions defensive wars might still occur. This modification of medieval Catholic doctrine is justified according to this view by the fundamental change in the character of modern warfare. In other quarters similar trends in thinking can be noted. Nevertheless, the limited validity of this argument must be recognized, since its basis is not the absolute evil of all war, but certain pragmatic considerations according to which in its present extreme form it has become too costly and dangerous. The moral issue is thus obscured. Furthermore such reasoning tends to exaggerate the distinction, qualitatively speaking, not only between offense and defense but also between earlier and present wars. Whether there exists a difference other than quantitative between the sacked cities of the Crusades and Hiroshima is not self-evident. At any rate, though every contribution which this theory can make to the prevention of war is to be welcomed, we dare not forget that rejecting war because it no longer "pays," no more constitutes Christian pacifism than being honest because it is the best policy, makes an honest man.

d. The concept of Christian pacifism as a vocation

Since the gathered character of the early church began to disappear, the discrepancy between the Christian ideal and the conduct of the nominally Christian masses has disquieted the earnest disciple. The resultant monasticism eventually led to a normalized dualistic social structure of the Christian community, while a dualistic ethic distinguished between the *consilia*, which constituted the maximal monastic norm, and the *praecepta*, which constituted the minimal norm of the masses. Against this dichotomous ethic the Reformation protested vigorously, but it still moved fully in the ethical atmosphere of the *corpus christianum*. Luther, for instance, in his concept of the two kingdoms, transferred this ethical tension from the social community into the anguished breast of the individual Christian. The Christian now followed, as it were, the *consilia* in his private life, while in political or military matters he maintained his former conduct which had supposedly met the demands of the *praecepta*. And so the Christian still serves in the army today: privately the *consilia* forbid him to kill, but the *praecepta* permit him to do so at the bidding of the state.

This same sort of dichotomy appears in the current view that God may call certain people to the pacifist position, just as he may call certain others to be preachers or teachers, or may give some other *charism*. Since their 16th-century dissent from this Reformation view, pacifist churches have held that this dichotomy belongs, not between higher and lower Christians, but between Christian and non-Christian, between church and world, where the New Testament placed it originally. We therefore reject the concept of vocational pacifism, which is the view often taken of our position by those who can neither accept nor reject it; for this concept is essentially a monastic one. While there is not only a place but also an urgent need for prophetic effort in the promotion of peace, we must maintain firmly that to put pacifism aside as a special calling for a few to keep the conscience of Christendom alive is a misinterpretation of the gospel ethic.

e. An antinomian concept of grace

It has been felt by some that the absolutist position of the pacifist represents a return to legalism inconsistent with Christian justification by faith, and that it creates a delusion of innocence equivalent to self-righteousness. On the other hand, it is assumed that the true Christian who admits his sin in going to war, and yields to God in penitence, is justified by God's grace. We readily admit that pacifism can contain elements of self-deception, legalism, and hypocrisy, and that pacifists can mistakenly suppose that they have fulfilled their responsibility simply by refusing to fight. But such dangers beset all areas of Christian living and are not peculiar to pacifists. The charge laid against pacifists seems rather to be based on two serious misreadings of the New Testament view of law and grace. First, since we are justified by faith and free from the law it is assumed that we are no longer subject to absolute norms but rather make our choices in the freedom of Christ, so that what may be sin for one need not be sin for another, since all live above the law. Now there is an element of truth in this view, for indeed we meet God no longer on the level of human merit and legalism but of grace; the power of sin and the judgment of the Mosaic law against us have been nullified; by writing the law in our heart God has placed us above it so that we obey because we will, not because we must. Nevertheless it is fundamentally false in supposing that the absolutes of the divine will are in any way suspended. Every man is still responsible to God for his works, good or bad.

In the second place, the above accusations seem unwarrantedly free in their application of grace. "What should we say then? Should we remain in sin so that grace may be given the more fully? Out of the question! We have died to sin; how could we go on living in it?" (Rom. 6:1, 2, NJB). "For there is no longer any sacrifice that will take away sins if we purposely go on sinning after the truth has been made known to us" (Heb. 10:26, TEV). Does not the assumption that we can deliberately go to war, because we go penitently realizing it to be sin, constitute a most serious abuse of the doctrine of grace? Can we really countenance the many conference resolutions that never go beyond the meaningless admonition that when we are implicated in a war we must at least fight penitently? As Christian pacifists we realize keenly that only by the grace of God and not through our pacifism can we stand in his sight. But we realize with equal keenness that justification is the door to a discipleship from which there is no turning back, and that deliberate sin nullifies the efficacy of grace for us.

f. The concept of war as the lesser evil

A very current line of nonpacifist reasoning regards war as a lesser evil than conquest and oppression. War is thus envisaged as a resistance to enemy invasion. Apart from the fact that this is obviously not a true picture of the behavior of both sides in all wars, we note at the outset that a valid comparison must be between two things of the same kind: it is valid to compare the infliction of one evil with the infliction of another, or the suffering of one evil with the suffering of another, but it has no moral meaning to say that one evil which a man may inflict is greater or less than another evil which he may suffer. If therefore this concept of the "lesser evil" means that a nation will inflict less evil on its enemies if it goes to war with them than it will suffer if it does not, it may or may not be a correct prediction, but in any case it gives no moral justification for going to war.

If the concept is taken as a comparison of two evils of which one or the other is to be suffered, it means that a nation will suffer less evil if it resists the invaders than if it does not. This may be true if it turns out that the defenders win the war, but it takes no account of the possibility that they may lose the war and so suffer not one of the two evils but both. In any case it is a purely prudential calculation, and as such it offers no guidance on the moral question whether it is or is not right to resort to war. The avoidance of suffering is no criterion of good: on the contrary, we are warned, as disciples of Jesus, to expect suffering, and we know that our free acceptance of suffering may have a redemptive value that no positive action of ours could have had.

To have any moral significance, the concept of the *lesser*

evil must be intended as a comparison of evils inflicted, either directly or indirectly, on others. It may be a quantitative comparison, meaning that although resorting to war admittedly inflicts suffering on one's enemies, this is less than the suffering of one's friends under enemy oppression, for which one would be responsible in refusing to go to war. Or it may be a qualitative comparison, meaning that it is a less evil thing to inflict suffering on one's enemies than to allow it to be inflicted on one's friends. Whichever kind of comparison it is, it means that he who resorts to war does evil, but he who does not does a greater evil, and thus the only choice is between two evil courses of action. This apparent inevitability of sin is expressed, in somewhat different terms, in the Oxford declaration:

> In all situations the Christian has to bear in mind both the absolute command, "Thou shalt love thy neighbor as thyself," and the obligation to do what most nearly corresponds to that command in the circumstances confronting him. His action may be but a poor expression of perfect love; the man is caught in a sinful situation, to the evil of which he may have contributed much or little. The best that is possible falls far "short of the glory of God" and is, in that sense, sinful; each man must bear his share of the corporate sin which has rendered impossible any better course; and we all have to confess that "our righteousnesses are as filthy rags." Yet to do what appears as relatively best is an absolute duty before God, and to fail in this is to incur positive guilt (178, 179-Ox).

This statement no doubt reflects faithfully the thinking of many, perhaps the majority of Christians, who assume that in our world of mutually related values ethical absolutes can be applied only relatively and that consequently the norm of conduct is not the absolute good but the "relatively best." In this way war, while wrong in an absolute sense, is thought to be the relatively best course in a particular situation. Sober reflection, however, will indicate at once that such an ethic moves on an entirely different level from that proclaimed by Christ.

To admit the possibility that a man may be placed in a position where he has no choice but to sin is to shut God out of his own world. We are God's children, and it is inconceivable that our Father, who loves us and wants us to behave as his children, could ever so abandon us. Christ himself, when seemingly faced with the choice of imposing his leadership by violence or permitting the extinction of his nascent kingdom, did not justify violence as a lesser evil, as the relatively best course, or as a means to a good end: he chose the way of God's will and his own nature, even though it was the way of the cross. And by that choice there came a release of God's power that could have come in no other way, and the situation was startlingly transformed so that the way that Christ chose was not after all the way to the extinction of his kingdom but the way, and the only way, to its triumph.

While we may recognize that human conduct does not attain absolute perfection in this life, such recognition is entirely different from the deliberate postulation of ethical norms different from those set up by Christ, or the admission that obedience is a relative matter. That certain absolutes apply to our own time is the obvious intent of Christ as seen in the Scriptures.

Even though we cannot achieve absolute perfection as human mortals, the only star given us to steer by is the perfect will of God.

g. The compatibility of war with Christian love

Some hold that a Christian spirit of love toward the enemy may be maintained even in the act of killing. But such a benevolent sentiment, even if it could be preserved by the killer, is not love, for "love worketh no ill" (Rom. 13:10, KJV). Furthermore a "love" that expresses itself in violence is for the victim indistinguishable from hatred, and can only call forth hatred and violence in return. Indeed, the higher the values in the name of which violence is done, the deeper will be the resentment of the victims against the "love" that kills them or their loved ones. The unhappy effect of colonial exploitation on Christian missions is sufficient demonstration that according Christian sanction to violence compromises the communication of the Gospel of love.

III. The Christian Nonresistant Pacifist Position
a. Love and the way of the cross

Christians all agree that the essence of the gospel is the love of God reaching down to redeem and transform the imperfections and sin which mar the life of men, and further, that this love must call forth in man a like expression of redemptive love for his fellowman. "This is my commandment, that you love one another as I have loved you" (John 15:12, RSV).

Those who read the New Testament in this perspective will find themselves in agreement with the numerous competent Christian scholars who have examined the passages commonly quoted in discussion of the peace and war issue, studying them objectively and with no attempt to read meanings into them. They will recognize that the words and spirit of the gospels fully warrant the Amsterdam statement that "war is incompatible with the teaching and example of Christ"; furthermore, that the cross of Christ, the heart of our faith, the means by which God's love operates redemptively in a world of sin, speaks against war, for it stands for the acceptance of unlimited suffering, the utter denial of self, and the complete dedication of life to the ministry of redemption.

But that cross is not merely exemplary, nor is the love to which it gives expression only redemptive, for beyond the cross lies the resurrection, and the moral renewal of the believer, "so that as Christ was raised from the dead by the Father's glorious power, we too should begin living a new life" (Rom. 6:4, NJB). Thus through the Scriptures and the light of Christ shining into the human heart man is made aware of the vital distinction in the sight of God between good and evil, right and wrong: aware that the problem of good and evil is bound up with the problem of his relationship with his brother; and aware increasingly that the overcoming of evil with good and the establishment of relationships of love and cooperation with his fellowman are possible to him only by the power of God working within him. The clear teachings of Christ: "Love your enemies"; "Do good to them that hate you"; "Resist not evil"; etc., bear the unmistakable authority both of his spoken Word as recorded in Scripture and of the inner witness of his Spirit. The Sermon on the Mount is in spirit declarative as well as imperative—such *is* the natural conduct of the children of God.

These assertions do not mean that we can achieve an easy perfection nor do they assume that human endeavor alone can bring about a warless world within history. Sin and violence will remain with us as long as man continues to abuse his moral freedom. The Christian himself is still subject to sin and to human limitation and still beset by the violence of the world. It is only the miracle of divine love that lifts him up, enabling him to realize the divine purpose of his existence. But he cannot claim that love without accepting the discipleship it entails with all its consequences. It is the heart of our position that once having been laid hold of by God through Christ the Christian owes him unqualified obedience. He may not calculate in advance what this may mean for himself or for society and obey only so far as seems practicable. The Christian is thus placed in a position of inevitable and endless tension.

Though he lives in the world and participates in the activities that belong to human life, he must recurrently face situations where loyalty to Christ, to the new *aeon* in which he already stands, means refusal to the world, *in which* he is, but *of which* he is not. Perhaps nowhere does this conflict of loyalties become more articulate or more acute than in the question of war. But here as elsewhere in life the Christian has but one weapon, to "overcome evil with good." His whole life must be one of unflinching fidelity to the way of redemptive love, even though it be the way of the cross.

b. The church

In his discipleship, however, the Christian is not an isolated individual whose faith is a matter merely of private interest. He is a member of the church, the universal community established by Christ in which his Spirit must reign and his will must be done, and from which must go out into all society the saving and healing ministry of the gospel. "Nothing stood out more clearly in the thought and work of the Oxford Conference than the recognition that the church in its essential nature is a universal society, united in its one Lord, and that in Him there can be neither Jew nor Greek, Barbarian nor Scythian, bond nor free" (31-Ox). Further, "the church should witness in word, in sacramental life, and in action to the reality of the kingdom of God which transcends the world of nations" (183-Ox). In her transcendent life the church already lives in the new aeon which she is called to manifest. As his body she lives according to the new "law of liberty," and we who are her members are called to "stand fast . . . in the liberty wherewith Christ hath made us free" (Gal 5:1, KJV), a freedom which no exercise of earthly authority can ever impair or usurp. Her source of life is the final and absolute reality of God in Christ, who in her existence manifests that power which will ultimately triumph over all the forces of darkness. To her has been entrusted the ministry of reconciliation, and henceforth neither she nor her members can engage in activities contrary to that mission. She is the herald of the new order, the kingdom of God, and her members must live within that order. Where in the supposed interest of the new order they revert to the methods of violence characteristic of the old they thwart the very process of redemption to which as Christians they are dedicated, for righteousness cannot spring up from unrighteousness, nor love from strife.

For Christians to allow themselves to be drawn into taking sides in war is a denial of the unity of the body of Christ. The Christian church is not provincial or national, it is universal. Therefore every war in which churches on each side condone or support the national effort becomes a civil war within the church. Is not this state of affairs where Christian kills Christian an even greater breach of ecumenical fellowship than the deplorable confessional differences that have rent our unity? Indeed, can we Christians expect the Lord to restore our unity in worship as long as we put one another to death on the field of battle? Therefore we humbly submit: The refusal to participate in and to support war in any form is the only course compatible with the high calling of the church of Jesus Christ.

c. Church and state

The church has to fulfill her mission not in a perfect society but in a world of men and nations who are free to spurn the will of God, in an aeon which Scripture itself recognizes will be marked by the continuing presence of evil. In the face of social disharmony both the Old and the New Testament recognize the authority of the state, as instituted to maintain order by force. This seeming contradiction of the ethic of love is clearly the heart of the problem of the Christian attitude toward war.

The classic New Testament passage dealing with this question, Romans 13, says unequivocally that the state is "ordained of God" as an institution of order, whose responsibility is the promotion of the good in society and the suppression of evil. Paul even concedes to the magistrate who bears the sword the lofty title, "minister of God." Acceptance of and obedience to the state is hence a matter of conscience. It is true that the state, particularly as we know it today, performs a host of other functions not connected with the execution of justice but salutary and necessary to society. But whatever may be the desirability of these functions in terms of political philosophy, the primary task of the state is still to be guarantor of order, the role in which it is a "minister of God to thee for good."

In the same breath, however, this passage asserts that "there is no power but of God." The state has therefore only a delegated and limited authority. It possesses nothing of a mystical or metaphysical quality, no autonomous norms or existence, no ultimate source of justice. Indeed this passage appears in a context where Paul had quoted God's words from the Song of Moses, "Vengeance is mine, I will repay" (Deut. 32:35, Rom. 12:19). Thus it is clear that whatever authority the state exercises, whatever justice it may be called upon to achieve, is purely of a delegated, relative, and provisional nature. At no point may its functions presume a suspension of the divine will.

Furthermore, the New Testament, and particularly the Apocalypse, sees in the state also a demonic quality. In this respect it is implicated in the usurped temporal power of the "prince of this world." This element, like a dominant trait in a biological organism, constantly seeks to assert itself, and leads a state, particularly one whose power is growing, to overstep its boundaries, to forget its derivative character, and to abuse its authority, as for example in the prosecution of modern warfare. In the eschatological vision of Scripture the kingdoms of this world are therefore visited with the righteous wrath of God. The authority which they are given becomes the very occasion of their downfall, and ultimately every functionary of the state stands before God as any other individual. For him therefore to kill men on the field of battle at the state's behest does not divest the deed of its sinful character, even though it appears to be a sin less heinous than private murder.

In the Old Testament, the first clear reference to the institution of justice in human hands follows the Noachian flood, where God declares: "If anyone sheds the blood of man, by man shall his blood be shed" (Gen. 9:6, NAB), stating thus a maxim later formulated as "Eye for eye, tooth for tooth" (Exod. 21:24). In the course of Jewish history, God appears to legitimatize military action, in contrast to his own prohibition of murder: "You shall not kill" (Ex. 20:13, NJB). But these behests stood in the context of human disobedience, where the people of Israel had to bear the consequences of their own wrongdoing. The resulting bloodshed was thus not God's original will for man but rather his judgment on human disobedience, whereby "sin was chastened by sin." We see this clearly in the great drama of Old Testament nations (e.g., Isa. 10), where God uses the spontaneous evil designs of one nation to punish another only for the first to fall under divine judgment itself, often for that very act, even though he had made it subserve his purposes. This principle is still operative today in the achieving of justice and order on the level of divine preservation, on which level war occurs. Here we stand before that humanly impenetrable mystery whereby the wrath of men, while judged by God, is nevertheless so diverted as to serve his glory, a mystery which we encounter even more strikingly in the crucifixion itself.

The role which war plays in the Old Testament has been a source of difficulty for many people, particularly for those who are most deeply convinced of the unity of the holy Scriptures. On the other hand the Old Testament especially has been a source book for many who have sought or felt called to give religious sanction to military enterprise. Obviously the various parts of the Bible cannot be examined here in regard to this question. The basic problem, however, constituted by the seeming contradiction between the Old and the New Testaments, finds its answer in the progression of redemptive revelation which culminated in Christ and in the corresponding progressive preparation of man for his advent. The pre-Christian covenants provided for man's provisional pardon, but they did not alter his fallen state. When Christ said, "Ye have heard that it hath been said," he referred to the old dispensation, where provisional justice and order were achieved through the natural laws of "eye for eye" and "tooth for tooth," although this was contrary to God's real intent then as now. But for those who have been renewed and placed into the new dispensation he goes on to prescribe a wholly different sort of conduct. "I tell you: do not take revenge on someone who wrongs you. . . . Love your enemies" (Matt. 5:39, 44, TEV). In the new economy of grace this vicious cycle of human sin is broken; henceforth the Christian is restored from his sinful state and is lifted into the new aeon, "into the glorious liberty of the children of God" (Rom. 8:21, KJV).

A distinction hereby becomes apparent between the dispensation of providence on the one hand, where violence, including that exercised by the state, remains embedded in the structure of unredeemed society, and the dispensation of redemption on the other, where man is restored to unity with God and made "a new creation": where "the old order is gone and a new being is there to see" (2 Cor. 5:17, NJB), where he cannot "continue in sin" because he is "dead" to it (Rom. 6:1-2, KJV). There is no provision for the Christian to revert, under force of circumstance, to the sub-Christian code of conduct. Hence it is clear that man's primary responsibility to God may never be annulled by the claims of the state. Under no circumstances, according to our understanding, may the Christian take the life of his fellow man, who also was created in the image of God and for whom Christ died.

War therefore presents itself to the Christian as a two-dimensional problem, not only because he himself stands in two "worlds," but also because in another sense the state too is of a dual character. In keeping with his conscientious affirmation of the state, he seeks through every legitimate secular or political means to help build the kind of society which can avoid war. Moreover, with war and its origin so intricately interwoven in the texture of social and particularly of economic life, the Christian conscience cannot renounce war while tolerating other abuses equally incompatible with the Christian ethic. In the highest sense, however, the Christian must regard his direct economic and political efforts as secondary, inasmuch as they are at best ameliorative and can never deal with the ultimate root of war, which is in the perverted human personality. Consequently, paradoxical as it may seem, he entertains no utopian illusions that the ethic of the gospel will be applied in its real meaning in international affairs as long as men reject the basic claims of Christ, for their acceptance alone can produce that ethic as fruit.

It follows that the Christian endeavor to eliminate war by political and other secular means does not constitute the heart of the church's peace effort. The task of the church does not consist in the statements she makes on international affairs or in the influence she exerts on national policies. Whether or not the church and Christians engage in war is not dependent on whether or not war can be avoided. The church's most effective witness and action against war comes on a different level and consists simply in the stand she takes in and through her members in the face of war. Unless the church, trusting the power of God in whose hand the destinies of nations lie, is willing to "fall into the ground and die," to renounce war absolutely, whatever sacrifice of freedoms, advantages, or possessions this might entail, even to the point of counseling a nation not to resist foreign conquest and occupation, she can give no prophetic message for the world of nations. As the Oxford report stated so aptly in another connection, "The first duty of the church, and its greatest service to the world, is that it be in very deed the church" (57-Ox, already quoted).

Such a position will admittedly often be misunderstood by the world as negativism, evasion of responsibility, and even betrayal. Indeed this is precisely the point that even Christians find difficult to comprehend. We cannot hope to convince alone by appeal to reason, for the issue here is one of faith and obedience which the "natural man" cannot comprehend (1 Cor. 2:4, 14). We can, however, point out that it is not a question here of evading responsibility but one of correct diagnosis and remedy. Certainly the church is the first to oppose evil wherever it is found, but she cannot fight this spiritual battle with physical weapons. Even though the problem of society is not in all respects the same as the problem of the individual, it remains true that moral evil has no existence in a community except as the effect of the evil will of members of the community, and consequently that social evil cannot be resolved by violence. Whatever our theory of evil we know that in practice it lies in the heart of man. It is not something external to him which can be struck and smashed or carted away, or which can be destroyed by an atom bomb. The waging of war only aggravates and spreads the trouble, and the Christian must turn from this to the far more difficult and unpopular task of attacking evil at its root. The only way to end war is to cease to fight, for the devil cannot be driven out by Beelzebub.

IV. The Common Christian Task

In this statement we have endeavored to set forth briefly the attitude of the Christian gospel toward war and to consider the present practices of the Christian church in the light of her professed faith. Our conclusion is that the church must reject war, not merely because of the disorder, waste, or suffering which it causes, but far more because it is contrary to the will of God. War is the negation of the gospel itself, of the great redemptive truths proclaimed through the centuries by the church, and of the ministry of reconciliation entrusted to her by her Master. We have seen further that "the first duty of the church to the world is to be the church," that the source of her strength and of her impact on world affairs is not the ability to out-maneuver the world at its own game, using the world's methods, but in the fact that she is, for all her weakness, the instrument of God, the body of Christ, the temple of the Holy Spirit. We have seen that Christians serve society not by being assimilated into society, but by being the salt of the earth and letting their light shine before men. Finally we have seen that the ultimate destiny of nations lies beyond human control, that whatever responsibility we carry, it is God who "makes and unmakes kings" (Dan. 2:21, NJB), and therefore the power of prayer and the working of God's Spirit through the faith and obedience of his servants are the only effective weapons against the forces of evil. If the church is impotent in this time of crisis, it is as a judgment on her lack of faith, because she still compromises and even denies her own intrinsic nature—declining to follow her Lord to suffering and the cross.

The World Council said at Amsterdam in 1948, "The part which war plays in our present international life is a sin against God and a degradation of man" (89-A). The reasoning by which, in spite of this admission of its sinfulness, Christians continue to justify participation in war is based on presuppositions which we have seen to be questionable. If such reasoning leads us to persist in what we have admitted to be sin, for the sole reason that the ethic of the gospel seems unrealistic, do we not behave as though this were not God's world, as though Christ had never given the church his Holy Spirit? The confession that Jesus Christ is Lord proclaims that God in Christ has created new possibilities which are not nullified by the Christian's involvement in sinful society. We are never so involved in sin that it is impossible for us to return, never so lost in the maze that God cannot lead us out again. The prophetic exhortations to repentance which we find recorded in Scripture never promised that the way of obedience would be easy, or that to take it would avoid all personal and national loss; but they always insisted that there was a way. We affirm that Christ is that way; and that in this world of tension and these times of strife the only course compatible with the prophetic calling of the Christian church is to renounce every complicity with materialism and national ambition, beginning with the rejection of war and refusing arms even for the defense of those values that the gospel has produced in our civilization. Let her whose very being is of the Spirit cast aside the unbelief of despair together with the unbelief of trust in violence, and place full faith in the weapons of her warfare, which are not carnal but mighty, in the resources of mercy and power which are hers by grace.

We believe that God has set no limits to the new possibilities that would be given the church to reconcile, to create, to pioneer; to relieve suffering, to alleviate tensions, and to meet every human need with the love of the gospel. Christians more than anyone else can bring to the social and political tensions which trouble our world a spirit of understanding, of patient and sacrificial concern for all men. In this spirit there can develop new processes of mediation and negotiation for the peaceful settlement of disputes. In this spirit the church can expand the help which she is already giving to the needy people of the world to overcome hunger, disease, and illiteracy, and can arouse the conscience of men and nations to direct to this purpose resources now squandered in a never-ending arms race. A world church entirely committed to a creative Christian pacifism could bring into world affairs a transformation as yet unimagined. Her own renunciation of warfare in favor of faith in the power of the Spirit would for the first time entitle her to call the nations to the act of faith which disarmament requires. We do not believe that war is inevitable, that it comes and goes as by an inexorable and arbitrary decree of fate. It cannot be avoided by armed might nor by compromise with evil, but only by the penitence, the faith, the obedience, the righteousness, and the love that exalt a nation. Ultimately God controls and shapes the destiny of nations, in accordance with their response to his will, and he dwells, not with the "biggest battalions" as was once blasphemously suggested, but "with the crushed and dejected in spirit" (Isa. 57:15, NAB).

Finally, our plea is not a utilitarian one; it is not based on the calculation that war will be eliminated at once if the church refuses to participate. We do not know "the times or dates the Father has set by his own authority" (Acts 1:7, NIV). But we do know assuredly from the promise of our Master that the gates of hell cannot prevail against the church and that therefore her victory cannot be measured in terms of military victory, nor her survival by the survival of a civilization. Our faith rests alone in "Christ who is both the power of God and the wisdom of God. God's folly is wiser than human wisdom, and God's weakness is stronger than human strength" (1 Cor. 1:24-25, NJB).

APPENDIX B

The Church, The Christian, and War

A Pacifist Statement by Seventy-eight Christian Leaders

Editor's Note:

*In late 1947 A. J. Muste recommended to the Fellowship of Reconciliation (FOR) National Council that leading church people from around the world submit to the upcoming Amsterdam Assembly a strong statement on the Christian pacifist attitude toward war. George A. Buttrick, Minister of Madison Avenue Presbyterian Church in New York City, wrote the statement which was signed by seventy-eight theologians and church leaders. The statement was sent to delegates and alternates just prior to the Assembly. It was also submitted as a memorandum to Commission IV, on "The Church and International Affairs," of the Assembly. The text reproduced here in its entirety was first published in **Fellowship**, the journal of Fellowship of Reconciliation, September 1948, vol. XIV, no. 8, pp. 17-24.*

Introduction

The Call to the Churches announcing the First Assembly of the World Council of Churches to be held in Amsterdam in August 1948 states the main theme before the Assembly to be Man's Disorder and God's Design, and says:

The design of God declares itself in the new environment for our lives that has been created by the acts of God in Christ. In this life, death and resurrection, and in the coming of the church, a new beginning has been made in human history. "What is old has gone, the new has come."

Confessing that the churches "have been partakers in man's disorder" the Call voices the hope that

> With the blessing of God, this Assembly can mark a new experience of the glory of God, and a new acceptance by Christians and Christian churches of their responsibility for seeking continually to bring the whole of human life and relations under the Kingship of Christ. . . . We long for the day when the Lord Jesus Christ shall recapture the churches and manifesting his glory, lead them to speak with one clear voice and to act as those who serve him only as their Lord.

Among the appalling manifestations of "man's disorder" is the evil of war. If "God's design" for human society is even in some slight measure to be restored in our age, this evil must be abolished. In order that this may be accomplished, it is clearly essential that on this subject of war and participation in it on the part of the churches and their members, the churches should now speak, under the guidance of the Holy Spirit, "with one clear voice."

The Oxford (1937) World Conference declared in its message to the Christian churches:

> The Universal Church, surveying the nations of the world, in every one of which it is now planted and rooted, must pronounce a condemnation of war unqualified and unrestricted. War can occur only as a fruit and manifestation of sin. This truth is unaffected by any question of what may be the duty of a nation which has to choose between entry upon war and a course which it believes to be a betrayal of right, or what may be the duty of a Christian citizen whose country is involved in war. The condemnation of war stands, and also the obligation to seek the way of freeing mankind from its physical, moral and spiritual ravages.

Section VII of the Message and Decisions of Oxford, entitled "The Church and War," reaffirmed this unequivocal condemnation of war:

> War involves compulsory enmity, diabolical outrage against human personality, and a wanton distortion of the truth. War is a particular demonstration of the power of sin in this world, and a defiance of the righteousness of God as revealed in Jesus Christ and him crucified. No justification of war must be allowed to conceal or minimize this fact.

The Section then proceeded to deal with the "agonizing perplexity" in which the Christian is involved as he seeks "to bear in mind both the absolute command, Thou shalt love thy neighbor as thyself, and the obligation to do what most nearly corresponds to that command in the circumstances confronting him." It called attention to the fact that there are widely divergent views in the churches regarding participation in war.

Oxford, however, pointed out that the church "cannot rest in permanent acquiescence in the continuance of these differences, but should do all that is possible to promote the study of the problem by people of different views meeting together to learn from one another as they seek to understand the purpose of God as revealed in Jesus Christ."

Since these words were written the world has passed through the experience of global war, occupation, resistance, and emergence of atomic weapons. We are confronted with the complete collapse of efforts to make the peace, with an atomic armaments race and the waging of a cold war between two rival powers which now largely dominate the earth.

Under these circumstances it would seem necessary and inevitable that a restudy and a further definition of the Christian attitude toward war be undertaken at the Assembly of the World Council of Churches at Amsterdam in August 1948 and in the discussions leading up to that Assembly. The undersigned are convinced that these discussions, if they are to have our Lord's blessing, must proceed in that spirit of Christian love, unity, and humility which Oxford enjoined upon the church and all its members and which the Call to the Amsterdam Assembly invokes. In this spirit and with the prayer that it may in some measure contribute to the achievement of our Lord's purpose "that they all may be one," the following statement is submitted for consideration and adoption at Amsterdam.

I

"God's Design" has been revealed in Christ. This revelation has three main aspects: incarnation, atonement, and resurrection. The relation of the church and of the Christian to war ought to be determined by these basic elements of the Christian faith.

The incarnation is the fact that God himself has fully entered history in Christ and there disclosed his nature and will. Revelation is thus ultimate and cannot appeal to any standard beside itself. The incarnation thus repudiates all historical relativisms which deny the availability of absolute authority and standards.

The atonement reveals the divine method of overcoming evil and redeeming sinners. The God who is absolute love became flesh in his Word to effect through the cross the eternal fellowship which is his historic purpose in Christ Jesus. In the life of Jesus, and above all in the cross which sealed it, a characteristic way of meeting and overcoming evil is revealed. Jesus never belittled or condoned the stark reality of evil, but he never met it with its own weapons. He overcame evil with good. This positive redemptive method of overcoming evil found its supreme climax in the cross, which Jesus deliberately willed to endure rather than prove false to that chosen redemptive way.

The resurrection declared that Christ is victor over the law, sin, and death. God waits for man to avail himself by faith and obedience, in all areas of life, of the fruits of his victory. Though human history is but part of the total drama, the resurrection applies to this history.

The Christian church is the body of Christ, the communion of those who believe in the incarnation, atonement, and resurrection. God is still in history, through Christ, as the Holy Spirit by means of the church. The church is a fellowship of forgiveness and redemptive concern, a supranational community, grounded in the supernatural order and revealing the continuous victory of the resurrection by the power of its faith, its witness, and its spiritual fruits.

The revelation in Christ also discloses the nature and purpose of the created order. History and nature, too, are God's means of creating fellowship whereby he indirectly conditions and controls the destiny of man without directly determining it. In the long past, this order of creation is God's indirect conditioning and control of man's responsible freedom, leading him to seek a better fellowship beyond the contradictions he experiences within the order of need, law, sin, judgment, and death.

The State's "God-given" Function

The state has, at least in our stage of history, a God-given function. All church members have therefore also a duty, as citizens, to the state, and, as children of God, for the state. On the other hand, the state is subject to the law and judgment of God.

Because the church evolves as an institution in history it participates, as does the individual Christian, in both the orders of redemption and creation. Yet the church is an act of the Holy Spirit, the body of Christ, and it exists primarily and distinctively in the order of redemption.

Because man has made sinful use of his freedom, the order of creation is actually characterized by sinful refusal of fellowship—hatred, violence, war—and by perversions of fellowship, and by partial, unsatisfactory fellowship. Nevertheless, God's authority is supreme, both in the order of creation and in the order of redemption. In Christ God's concern for the creation of a rich and free fellowship among men is revealed. The whole material and historic realm was ordained of God as a means to the realization of this fellowship and a medium for its expression.

The church, therefore, must not become conformed to this world. "If the salt have lost its savour . . . it is thenceforth good for nothing." The church in the name of its Lord must judge the world both by its message and its stand, its word and its works. Above all, it must be a saving and redemptive power in and for the world. The order of creation must be increasingly lighted and led by the order of redemption. "The works that I do shall ye do also."

Even though true church members are more conscious of sin and the need of forgiveness than others, this consciousness and the fact that they participate also in a sinful order must never, therefore, make them deny the presence of the Holy Spirit in history. Even though the leaven has not leavened the whole lump, it is still leaven; and by becoming more potent it can in God's time and by his grace leaven the lump.

Highest Duty to God

It follows that when duty to the state conflicts with the primary duty to God and to the nature and requirements of the Christian fellowship, duty to the state at this point becomes subordinate. From there on the sons of God exercise their freedom through their responsibility to God for the state. The fullest possible nonparticipation in the evil then becomes the strongest witness of the church and the Christian. True responsibility to the state is exercised by calling the state back from its defiance of God, its self-destruction and destruction of others.

Such nonconformity is possible and effective, as was demonstrated by Christians in the infancy of the church and as has been demonstrated in our own time by churches and their members who even in totalitarian states have disobeyed Caesar and refused to conform to his decrees.

Progress and the Conscience

Under the guidance, we believe, of the Holy Spirit, the Christian conscience has thus at various times become particularly sensitive upon a particular issue, because it has seen there an eruption-point of the forces of evil in their defiance of the law of God. It is precisely thus that the tension resulting from the humble and sincere effort to obey the absolute law of the kingdom in a world not wholly redeemed contributes to ethical progress.

Though seemingly foolish and impotent the church and its members thus become in the darkest hour channels through which the wisdom and power of God are released in history and evil is overcome. God's power is made perfect in weakness. In seeming to lose its life the church has found it and has imparted new life to the world.

II

These considerations constitute the basis for Christian reflection upon the question with which we began: that of the attitude of the church and the Christian toward war in the light of the conditions under which we now live.

The true nature of modern war has now been revealed as unquestionably totalitarian and involving the elevation of military expediency to the supreme principle of human conduct in wartime. There is now no serious doubt among thinking people, whether in or out of the church, that war must be abolished if our civilization is to survive. It may be that the very survival of the human race on earth hinges upon the prevention of atomic and bacterial war. Nor do God and history give us unlimited time. The situation is as urgent as it is grave.

It is now obvious that efforts to set limits to war are futile, that the old measures to abolish war are inadequate, and that merely multiplying the energies devoted to such measures is entirely useless. Human wisdom has proved foolishness. The mightiest instruments of material power have become sources of insecurity and weakness. The world must be saved by the power and wisdom of God in Christ or it will perish. If in this hour the church of Christ has no distinctive message to the nations, if it does not lead them to a great act of reconciliation through faith in the power of the Spirit rather than the weapons of the flesh, an unprecedented catastrophe will overwhelm mankind. Our churches will stand under the terrible judgment of their crucified and risen Lord.

We are accordingly led to the following specific conclusions on the attitude of the church and the Christian toward war:

1. The church, which is the body of Christ, and the incarnation of the Holy Spirit, cannot ever be at war. The nature and function of the church to be a redemptive community inseparably uniting men in self-giving concern, and that of war which openly divides men by total conflict, are completely contradictory. Force which is susceptible of constructive employment for the common welfare roots back into the very nature of the created order. This in no wise alters the fact that the destructive and unrestrained violence of modern war is utterly inconsistent with the nature and task of the church.

Accordingly, when war is being waged, the church must first of all witness to the purpose of God in Christ Jesus by being radical itself. Its greatest service is to be alive in and demonstrate the power of a higher order of life than that of the secular society about it. It must be the universal, supranational fellowship of redemptive love which refuses to participate in violence and war. It cannot do otherwise and yet remain Christian.

2. From the nature and function of the church it follows also that the members of the church should not participate in war. Christians cannot love universally as church members and yet fight with each other as citizens. Christian citizens have real duties to the state, but their first duty is to Christ. When they cannot obey both God and country, their first duty is to God.

3. The church today must call upon peoples and governments, unitedly or singly, to cease from war and from war preparations, to abandon the weapons of mass destruction and to adopt peaceful procedures for the settlement of conflict and overcoming of tyranny or aggression. The church must not shrink from thus summoning all the nations and each nation to a radical repentance, to casting away the weapons of the flesh, to faith in the divine method of overcoming evil and reconciling men revealed in the cross, to the adoption of "God's design" for the ordering of the nation's and the world's life.

The church is worldwide and could creatively empower and guide the whole order of creation if the church were truly the church. As Christians, we have failed the world by remaining too much on its level in thought and action, doubting the power and love of God and not becoming increasingly baptized by the Holy Spirit to the bearing of rich spiritual fruits. We need true repentance and reformation. That could help the world by providing a steady light and a constant source of power.

Even if in this supreme crisis the church's being Christian should fail to affect substantially and desirably the life of our time, leading instead to her suffering and disdain, the issues of history are in God's hands and all we are bid is to be faithful.

SIGNED BY:
(Locations and titles are given for purposes of identification only. Signers have given their names in their individual and not their official capacities.)

Argentina
Sante U. Barbieri, Rector, Union Theological Seminary, Buenos Aires
Belgium
Jacques Harte, President, Conseil d' Eglise Cretienne Missionnaire
Philippe Vernier, Pastor, Quaregnon
Canada
Willard Brewing, Minister, St. George's United Church, Toronto
James T. Dawson, General Superintendent, British Methodist Episcopal Church
James M. Finlay, Minister, Carlton Street United Church, Toronto
Frederick W. Norwood, Minister, St. James United Church, Montreal
J. Lavell Smith, Superintendent, The Church of All Nations, Toronto.
Chile
Enrique C. Balloch, South American Bishop for Methodist Board of Foreign Missions
China
S. H. Fong, President, West China University, Chengtu
Liao Hung-Ying (Mrs. H. D. Bryan), British Council, Nanking
J. Usang Ly, Chairman of the National Committee, YMCA of China
Christopher Tang, Instructor of Church History, Nanking Theological Seminary
Wallace Wang, President, West China Union Theological College, Chengtu

Czechoslovakia
Five signers whose names are withheld
Denmark
Einar Ege, Dean, Cathedral of Roskilde
France
Rene Charras, Evangeliste, Free Church Mazet-St. Voy (Haute Loire)
Charles Delizy, Pastor, French Reformed Church, Freycenet (Haute Loire); President, Consistoire de la Montagne
Jacques Martin, Editor, "Christianisme Social"
Paul Ricoeur, Professor of Philosophy, engaged in research studies for the Ministry of National Education
Henri Roser, Chairman of Evangelism, Reformed Church
Edouard Theis, Director, College Cevenol, Le Chambon-sur-Lignon
André Trocmé, Pastor, Reformed Church, Le Chambon-sur-Lignon
Pierre Umdenstock, Pastor, Reformed Church, Tence (Haute Loire)
Germany
Rudolf Daur, Pastor, Evangelische Kirche im Deutschland, Stuttgart
Hermann Maas, Decanus, E.K.I.D., Heidelberg
Wilhelm Mensching, Pastor, E.K.I.D., Petzen bei Buckeburg
Harald Polchau, Pastor, E.K.I,D., Berlin; former Chaplain, Berlin-Tegel Prison
F. Siegmund-Schultze, Professor, University of Muenster
Great Britain
A. M. Chirgwin, General Secretary, London Missionary Society
Archibald C. Craig, Formerly General Secretary, British Council of Churches
H. H. Farmer, Professor Systematic Theology, Westminster College, Cambridge University
L. W. Grensted, Nolloth Professor of the Philosophy of the Christian Religion, University of Oxford
G. H. C. Macgregor, Professor of Biblical Criticism, University of Glasgow
D. M. Mackinnon, Regius Professor of Moral Philosophy, University of Aberdeen

George F. MacLeod, Iona Community, Scotland
Charles E. Raven, Master of Christ's College and Regius
	Professor of Divinity, University of Cambridge
William Robinson, Principal of Overdale College, Selly
	Oak, Birmingham

India

C. S. Paul, General Secretary, Student Christian Move-
	ment of India, Pakistan, and Ceylon

Japan

Iwawo Ayusawa, Formerly Under-secretary, International
	Labor Office, Geneva, Switzerland; Executive Direc-
	tor, Central Labor Relations Board, Japanese Gov-
	ernment
Toyohiko Kagawa, Preacher, Founder of Cooperatives,
	Author
Michi Kawai, Principal, Keisen Girls' School, Tokyo
Michio Kozaki, Moderator of the Church of Christ in Ja-
	pan
Tamaki Uemura, President, National Council YWCA of
	Japan

Netherlands

J. J. Buskes, Ned. Hervormde Kerk, Amsterdam
G. J. Heering, University of Leyden
M. Hinlopen, Ned. Hervormde Kerk, Amsterdam
T. O. Hylkema, Mennonites, Amsterdam
Kr. Stryd, Ned. Hervormde Kerk, s'Hertogenbosch

New Zealand

Alan A. Brash, General Secretary of the National Council
	of Churches in New Zealand; Secretary of the Na-
	tional Missionary Council
John Henderson, Professor of Theology and Church His-
	tory, Knox College; Dean of the Faculty of Theolo-
	gy, University of Otago, Dunedin

United States of America

Rufus D. Bowman, President, Bethany Biblical Seminary,
	Church of the Brethren
George A. Buttrick, Minister, Madison Avenue Presbyte-
	rian Church, N.Y.C.
Henry J. Cadbury, Divinity School of Harvard University;
	Chairman, American Friends Service Committee
Adelaide T. Case, Professor of Christian Education, Epis-
	copal Theological School, Cambridge, Massachu-
	setts

Edwin T. Dahlberg, former President, Northern Baptist
   Convention

Albert E. Day, Minister, Mount Vernon Place Methodist
   Church, Baltimore, Maryland

William J. Faulkner, Dean of Chapel, Fisk University,
   Nashville, Tennessee

Nels F. S. Ferré, Abbott Professor of Theology, Andover-
   Newton Theological Seminary, Newton Centre,
   Massachusetts

Elmer A. Fridell, Secretary for China, Japan, the Philip-
   pines, American Baptist Foreign Missionary Society

Elwood L. Haines, Bishop of Iowa, Protestant Episcopal
   Church

Kenneth Scott Latourette, Professor of Missions and Oriental History, Yale University; President, American
   Historical Association

E. K. Higson, Secretary, Department of Oriental Missions,
   United Christian Missionary Society of the Disciples
   of Christ

Paul S. Johnson, Professor of Psychology of Religion,
   Boston University School of Theology

William E. Lampe, Secretary, Evangelical and Reformed
   Church

W. Appleton Lawrence, Bishop of Western Massachusetts, Protestant Episcopal Church

Charles Tudor Leber, Secretary, Board of Foreign Missions, Presbyterian Church, USA

D. P. McGeachy, Minister, Presbyterian Church, U.S.,
   Clearwater, Fla.

William Stuart Nelson, Dean, School of Religion, Howard University, Washington, D.C.

Albert W. Palmer, Moderator, Congregational-Christian
   Churches, USA

Edwin McNeill Poteat, President, Colgate-Rochester
   Theological Seminary, Rochester, New York

Carl C. Rasmussen, Professor of Systematic Theology,
   Lutheran Theological Seminary, Gettysburg, Pennsylvania

F. P. Stocker, President, Provincial Elders' Conference,
   Moravian Church, Bethlehem, Pennsylvania

Ernest Fremont Tittle, Minister, First Methodist Church,
   Evanston, Illinois

APPENDIX C

40 Years of Ecumenical Theological Dialogue Efforts on Justice and Peace Issues by the Fellowship of Reconciliation And The "Historic Peace Churches"[9]

A chronology
compiled by John Howard Yoder[10]

The formal dialogues had a prehistory both in North America and in Europe. The "historic peace churches" of the U.S. and Canada have possessed a "continuation committee" for occasional liaison since a conference at North Newton, Kansas in 1935. The original committee functioned with special regard to problems concerning conscientious objection to military service. Three communions were represented in that liaison by the heads of their service agencies (the Mennonite Central Committee, the Brethren Service Committee, and the American Friends Service Committee). It did not include the Fellowship of Reconciliation nor did it take responsibility for communicating with nonpacifist Christians.

In the European prehistory of the dialogues Dr. F.

Siegmund-Schulze had a dual role. He was the main voice *both* of the ecumenical movement in process of becoming and of the International Fellowship of Reconciliation. Both agencies had arisen out of the collapse of the 1914 international conference for "Friendship Through the Churches," and many people were active in both.[11]

Chronology of the Formal Dialogues

1948 Commission IV of the First Assembly of the World Council of Churches held at Amsterdam in the Netherlands focused on "Man's Disorder and God's Design." Under the leadership of FOR (USA) 78 prominent churchmen from 15 nations submitted a statement to Commission IV, entitled "The Church—the Christian—and War." It is reproduced above as Appendix B.[12] The signers included one each of Brethren, Mennonites, and Friends, but not as official confessional representatives. At the request of FOR, George A. Buttrick, minister of Madison Avenue Presbyterian Church, wrote the draft. FOR collected the signatures including five anonymous ones from Czechoslovakia and five from continental China.

1948 The Amsterdam Assembly of the WCC accepted a statement from Section IV. One portion of it was called: "War Is Contrary to the Will of God." It described three mutually incompatible views held by Christians with regard to the morality of war, and concluded: "We must acknowledge our deep sense of perplexity in face of these conflicting opinions. . . . We believe that there is a special call to theologians to consider the theological problems involved."[13]

1949 At the Abbey of Présinge (near Geneva, Switzerland), a "continuation committee" for Europe was constituted in a May 5-7 meeting. Representing the Brethren Service Committee, Elgin, Illinois was M. Robert Zigler (then in Geneva). He had previously represented the Brethren on the North American continuation committee. The Peace Committee of London Yearly Meeting of Friends was represented by Eric Tucker. Percy Bartlett, another London Quaker, represented the International Fellowship of Reconciliation. The Peace Section of the Mennonite Central Committee, Akron, Pennsylvania, was represented by Harold S. Bender (at Basel 1948-1949), then Guy F. Hershberger (1949-1950), and then Irvin B. Horst (then in the Netherlands).

The Mennonite representation turned over every few years as different persons were given the part-time assignment by the MCC Peace Section. The other three agencies were represented by long-term Europe-based staff. The Mennonites of Europe and the Friends of North America were not formally represented, although Irvin Horst consulted with the Dutch Mennonites at important points in the process.

1949 A wider, get-acquainted meeting of personnel from the HPCs and FOR agencies was held at Heerewegen in the Netherlands, August 2-4. Its findings recommended common measures both for defending the rights of conscientious objectors and for communicating with "our non-pacifist brethren." More specifically, alluding to the Amsterdam Assembly's "special call to the theologians," they decided that "the WCC should be asked how far this study has been encouraged and has proceeded."

1950 The creation of a new instrument of ecumenical witness in North America, the Church Peace Mission began with a large conference in Detroit. Staffed by A. J. Muste (a Quaker working for FOR), but supported and governed by the HPCs, it represented a more "churchly" and theological image and commitment than characterized the FOR previously. It worked through large conferences like the one in Detroit and most notably in Evanston in 1959. It also worked through smaller study groups of scholars like the one who produced the book *Biblical Realism Confronts the Nation*, and pamphlets like: (1) "The Christian Conscience and War" published in 1959 with participation by 32 churchmen, (2) "The Church, the Christian, and the World," (3) "Christian Pacifism Today," and (4) the "Christian Approach to Nuclear War, 1960."

1951 The European continuation committee (henceforth EurCC), in a meeting at Heerewegen, Netherlands, in July, responding to letters addressed to M. Robert Zigler by the WCC's General Secretary, W. A. Visser 't Hooft, took steps to prepare and submit two statements:

(1) The case for the legal recognition of the right to conscientious objection: The door for this had been opened by the Toronto WCC Central Committee meeting, July 9-13, 1950. The statement was referred to the next Central Committee meeting. There it was said to have met opposition, especially from the Greek Orthodox, but it was acted on affirmatively by the Central Committee.[14]

(2) "War Is Contrary to the Will of God": This 7,000-word document was comprised of a brief statement from each of the HPCs and the FOR (the Mennonite part was contributed to by both Dutch and North American drafts) plus a common preface (DB: 47ff.). This text appealed directly to the "call to the theologians" mentioned in the Amsterdam Assembly text.

Although it would have been appropriate for this testimony to go to the Faith and Order Commission of the WCC, since it had to do with a matter of denominational identity, or to the Department of Studies it was referred instead to the Churches' Commission on International Affairs, the agency set up jointly by the WCC and the International Missionary Council to relate to the United Nations. Its head, C. J. Patijn, shrugged the statement off as unrealistic.

1952 In January, the EurCC met with W. A. Visser 't Hooft at the Abbey of Présinge (near Geneva). In addition to presenting a substantial paper on the ways in which the WCC contributed to peace, Visser 't Hooft said lightly: "If you can't get four basically agreed tiny groups to make a common statement, what do you want me to do with 150 churches?"

1952 EurCC planned an expanded meeting for Heerewegen in September to which a large number of youth from the volunteer services were to be invited. EurCC took up the challenge from W. A. Visser 't Hooft and asked Mennonite Paul Peachey to take editorial initiative in the writing project which led to "Peace Is the Will of God" (DB 73ff.), submitted to the WCC before the Second Assembly at Evanston, Illinois, in 1954.

1954 The Evanston Assembly spoke extensively on "Christians in the Struggle for World Community" (DB 92ff.) but did not face the classic debate about the morality of war as clearly as Amsterdam had. Pacifism was alluded to, not as a possible moral position over against other possible moral positions, but as "a mode of witness." Evanston, however, did give special attention to the advent of nuclear weapons.

1955 In an expanded meeting, March 22-23, at Geneva, the EurCC met with Robert Bilheimer, Studies Secretary of the WCC, asking how the HPCs and FOR could be helpful to the WCC in pursuing the question of the morality of war.

Bilheimer said that, realistically, by the nature of WCC politics, there could be no *direct* pacifist contribution. If, however, the peace people did a significant study of their own, and came up with notable results, the other churches and the WCC would have to take note.

In response to this challenge the EurCC convened a conference, "The Lordship of Christ over Church and State." To sponsor and plan the event, German Protestant leaders of the Niemoller school were recruited to the EurCC. The plans were coordinated by Oberkirchenrat Heinz Kloppenburg, whose assistance had been negotiated by A. J. Muste. The first meeting was held at Crêt Bérard retreat center in Puidoux (near Lausanne, Switzerland) August 15-19, 1955.

The objective of the Puidoux meeting was not to carry on a conversation with nonpacifists, but to develop a way for FOR/HPC spokespeople to express together a peace witness to nonpacifists. The leaders and representatives of the several groups, especially the North American Mennonites, were particularly aware of the differences among the four groups with regard to their modes of interpretation and witness. Rather than simply combine or average their different styles, the Puidoux study asked in what terms it would be best to address the nonpacifist communions. The German Protestants were invited as advisers to aid in this search for a common witness.

This meeting was marked by an especially appreciated encounter between the veterans of the Kirchenkampf (Kloppenburg, Ernst Wolf) and the theologians/historians of the Radical Reformation (Mennonite H. S. Bender, Quaker H. G. Wood).

From here the so-called Puidoux conference series continued with major gatherings (see below for details) at Iserlohn in 1957, Bievres in 1960, and Leiden in 1962. All were on the topic, "The Lordship of Christ Over Church and State."

Smaller "Puidoux meetings" were held between the above and continued even later: Vallecrosia, April 1956; Askov, August 1957; Hochst, January 1967, 1968, 1969; Gwatt, July 1970; Bienenberg, July 1973.

1955 Reinhold Niebuhr's biweekly *Christianity and Crisis*, vol. 15, no. 10 (June 13, 1955) published a statement, "God Wills Both Justice and Peace," signed by Niebuhr himself and by Episcopalian Bishop Angus Dun, responding to *Peace Is the Will of God*. It was rumored that WCC General Secretary Visser 't Hooft had insisted that the pacifist statement should not be left unanswered. Richard Fagley of the Commission of the Churches on International Affairs' New York Staff had assisted with the drafting (DB 100ff.).

1955 The Central Committee of the WCC authorized a study, "The Lordship of Christ Over the World and the Church." It was carried through by Study Department Secretary Hans Heinrich Harms with a commission of 21 male scholars, mostly biblical theologians, all of whom were from Western Europe and North America except for one Hungarian. They met twice, and had no connection with the HPCs/FOR, but the theme was close to the one with which the Puidoux series had begun.

1955 The 1955 Central Committee also mandated a study on "Christians and the Prevention of War in an Atomic Age" (excerpted in DB 185ff.). It was administered by Study Department Secretary Robert Bilheimer with a commission of 14 men, all West European and North American. One (Douglas V. Steere) was a Friend, two (Steere and Hannes de Graaf, Dutch Reformed) were IFOR leaders—but the FOR/HPC agencies had nothing to do with the process. The group met twice, and their report was an early statement of what was later called "nuclear pacifism." Although strong voices in the 1958 Central Committee tried to quash it, it was finally published by SCM Press in London in 1961.

1957 Puidoux II was held at Iserlohn West Germany, July 29-August 1, and produced "Discipleship as Witness to Unity in Christ" (DB 146ff.).

1958 The EurCC prepared a response to Dun and Niebuhr's "God Wills Both Justice and Peace." Its title was: "God Establishes Both Peace and Justice," and was written largely by Mennonites Paul Peachey and Albert Meyer along with British Friend Colin Fawcett (DB 108ff.).

1960 Puidoux III was held at Bievres (near Paris). It was one of the first West European ecumenical events to have sizable participation from Eastern Europe, including the planners of the Prague Christian Peace Conference (DB 196ff.).

1962 Puidoux IV, the last large conference in the Puidoux series, was held at Leiden. Its specific theme was "The Sources of Christian Social Ethics." Major conference papers were published by the WCC Division of Studies. The smaller study groups continued until 1973.

1965 At the Bossey Ecumenical Institute of the WCC in Switzerland a large conference was held June 28-July 3 on "God's Reconciling Work Among the Nations." Several Puidoux people participated; Heinz Kloppenburg was involved in the planning.

1968 At the Third WCC Assembly in 1961 in New Delhi a staff recommendation was approved which called for a small conversation between pacifist and nonpacifist theologians (DB 223). Nothing came of this recommendation until after all of the preparations for the Uppsala Assembly had been completed (DB 306). A meeting fitting the New Delhi description was then called by the Study Department (then headed by Victor Hayward) and was held at Bossey May/June 1968.

The pacifist side included Bo Wirmark (FOR Sweden), Heinold Fast (German Mennonite, Puidoux), and Mennonite John Howard Yoder.

The nonpacifist side was represented by some experienced ecumenical conference-goers who had never thought much about the matter of war and peace before. Like their predecessors they agreed that it is an important question worthy of more study (DB 306ff.). After the Uppsala Assembly the WCC was restructured in a way which eliminated the Study Department.

1968 The Fourth WCC Assembly at Uppsala adopted a Martin Luther King, Jr., Memorial Resolution calling for study of "nonviolent methods of social change." Wilmer Cooper (Friends United Meeting—FUM) and Barrett Hollister (Friends General Conference—FGC) with the aid of Martin Niemoller had the most to do with that Resolution's being passed. They kept in touch with each other and with the WCC staff to foster its implementation.

Their consultation together was at first quite informal, with Cooper convening and John Howard Yoder co-opted to the group. In time the process evolved into regular meetings of staff from the HPCs and FOR. This became known as the North American HPC/FOR Continuation Committee. FOR was represented from Nyack and both FGC and FUM Friends were involved. This liaison provided for consultation at the WCC Assemblies in Nairobi in 1975 and again at Vancouver in 1983.

To encourage and assist the projected WCC study, FGC

funded the preparation by Patricia Parkman of "A Proposal for Implementation of the Martin Luther King Resolution" (12pp., 1969) which included a "job description" and bibliography for the study and donated it to the WCC to demonstrate the feasibility of the study.

1970 Until 1970 nothing was done by the WCC with the "King Resolution." Then in the midst of the turmoil over the alleged "funding of revolution" by the WCC's Program to Combat Racism, the Central Committee authorized the study. It was implemented by David Gill, an Australian Methodist on the WCC staff, working half time for the two years 1971-1973. The most visible formal event within the study was a consultation at Cardiff, Wales, in September 1972 (DB 329). The NoAmerCC convened a group at Richmond, Indiana, December 1972, to study the Cardiff document (DB 353).

1973 The final report of the Gill study, *Violence, Nonviolence and the Struggle for Social Justice* was "commended by the Central Committee" in its meeting of August 1973 (DB 373ff).[15] By this time the staff was gearing up for the Fifth Assembly at Nairobi, and none of the actions recommended by the Gill report was implemented.

1975 Wilmer Cooper wrote a narrative review of the progress of the "King Resolution" for the Nairobi Assembly, which was entitled "Background Paper on the World Council Program on Violence, Nonviolence and the Struggle for Social Justice." It concluded, "Since David Gill completed the two-year study in 1972, very little of significance has happened . . . the original intent of the Martin Luther King Resolution has been blurred and for the most part overlooked."

A caucus of HPC/FOR people at Nairobi was convened

by FGC Delegate Lawrence McK. Miller, FOR's Richard
Deats, and Mennonite John H. Yoder. About a dozen
FOR/HPC people were at the Assembly. They met almost
daily to keep in touch with what was going on in the many
places in the program that could be of importance for a
peace witness. IFOR also arranged for a coffeehouse, near
the Assembly venue, with its own program (DB 386).

At Nairobi no direct attention was given to the moral issue of war in itself, an indication of progress backwards
since Oxford/Amsterdam. However, a proposal was made
for a "program to combat militarism" under CCIA auspices. NoAmerCC submitted two documents: (1) "Contributions of the HPCs on the Peaceful Resolution of Conflicts";
(2) "Contributions of the HPCs on Theological Issues Related to Militarism." The program as it was developed by
Geneva staff used the services of Ernie Regehr, Canadian
Mennonite, but was unrelated to the continuation committee structures.

Lamar Gibble, at the time serving as Church of the
Brethren representative on the NoAmerCC, was appointed
to the Commission of Churches on International Affairs.
There was, however, no formal relation to the NoAmerCC.

1981 An ad hoc "hearing" on nuclear weapons and disarmament was convened at Amsterdam by the WCC. It concluded "that the time has come when the churches must
unequivocally declare that the production and deployment
as well as the use of nuclear weapons are a crime against
humanity, and that such activities must be condemned on
ethical and theological grounds." Its report was entitled
Before It's Too Late. The WCC Central Committee made
this statement its own in 1982.

1983 The Lutheran Bishop of Stockholm, Olof Sundby,
convened an ad hoc conference in April on "Life and

Peace" supporting the Amsterdam statement. There was wide nonofficial participation from about 60 countries. The Life and Peace Institute was founded upon recommendation of this conference.

Ad hoc support came from other quarters when Patriarch Pimen of the Russian Orthodox Church convened a gathering May 10-14. It was titled "Religious Workers for Saving the Sacred Gift of Life from Nuclear Catastrophe." People from 90 countries and eight religions were represented.

The Christian Peace Conference, based in Prague, also contributed a statement that year.

1983 At the Sixth Assembly of the WCC in Vancouver, British Columbia, in August, a peace coffee-house was administered by the Canadian Ploughshares group. A series of FOR/HPC caucuses were held also.

The Interchurch Peace Council (Netherlands) and Ploughshares (Canada) took the lead in preparing and submitting a "Vancouver Appeal" signed by 19 dignitaries. They did not ask the WCC to take a pacifist position, but they did ask the WCC to support peacemaking activities around the world.

1983 The Vancouver Assembly spoke to the theme of peace specifically in three ways: (1) In Section 3.5 of the broad Assembly study process, a document, "Confronting Threats to Peace and Survival," was adopted. It repeated the Amsterdam 1981 declaration, and again stated that nuclear deterrence is morally unacceptable.

(2) A second "Statement on Peace and Justice" was prepared in the context of the Assembly's central steering process.

(3) Section 3.6 of the study process, headed "Struggling for Justice and Human Dignity," invited "churches at all

levels" to "enter into a covenant in a conciliar process . . . to work for justice and peace. . . ."

This proposal has since grown into a movement with a life and staff of its own. It is within but also extends beyond the WCC. The process it fosters under the heading "Justice, Peace, and the Integrity of Creation," culminated in a world convocation at Seoul, Southern Korea, March 6-12, 1990.

1985 The NoAmerCC initiated work on a response to the Vancouver Peace statements. A subcommittee was assigned the task of preparing a sequel to the 1953 declaration *Peace Is the Will of God*. Unlike that statement, the response is conceived as addressed to the worldwide Christian community. It seeks to avoid traditional sectarian modes of witness in favor of a more generally accessible biblical theological language.

1986 The staff assembled by the WCC to prepare the "preconciliar process" concerning "Justice, Peace, and the Integrity of Creation" convened a one-time consultation at Glion, Switzerland, in November. Stephen Cary (AFSC, FWCC), Hildegard Goss-Mayr (IFOR), and John Howard Yoder were among the resource persons invited ad hoc.

Notes

1. The four are identified in footnote 3.

2. The major documents, studies, and papers that facilitated and gave substance to the ongoing dialogue on war/peace from 1935 to 1975 are contained in *On Earth Peace*, ed. Donald F. Durnbaugh (Elgin, Ill.: Brethren Press, 1978). There are 26 separate documents in the 412 pages of this volume, still in print ($9.95 plus postage and handling). A number of consultations and conferences were held at places including Newton, Kan.; Crêt Bérard retreat center in Puidoux, Switzerland; Nairobi, Kenya; and New Windsor, Md.

The only meeting directly on the morality of war was a small consultation held at the WCC Ecumenical Institute in Bossey, Switzerland, in May 1968 (reported by Durnbaugh, pp. 307ff.). It concluded:

". . . we have confirmed the existence of a deep and genuine cleavage which is both theological and practical. New developments . . . do not render this issue obsolete, but rather heighten its relevance."

3. For half a century Mennonites, Friends (Quakers), and Brethren have been grouped together in ecumenical language as "historic peace churches." This usage arose in 1935 in the recognition that:

—each has been visibly active worldwide in relief for the victims of war and other kinds of service, and in fostering international communication;

—each has assumed or affirmed the supranational quality of Christian fellowship;

—each has historically taught that the Christian is called not to participate in war, even when required to do so by government.

The fourth participating body, the Fellowship of Reconciliation, is younger than the "historic peace churches," but older than their working together under that label. Founded in 1914 it is a transnational fellowship of local and national chapters and denominational fellowships who hold to pacifist convictions and support activities like those of the "HPCs."

It should be noted that FOR's participation in this and other ecumenical projects is on behalf of its members who are Christian. As an interfaith fellowship the FOR is composed of members of other faith traditions as well.

4. We follow the traditional usage of most Christians in using the term *war* here to designate the moral issue we address. Yet the moral judgment stated here on war must apply as well to judging some policies and practices which others would wish to designate as *peace* or as *justice*; especially

—escalating arms threats with the purported goal of deterrence;

—the militarization of domestic society, which some call "security;"

—lethal insurrections with the purported goal of some community's liberation;

—irregular forms of armed conflict, which some call "low intensity warfare."

5. See Appendix A, "Peace Is the Will of God," for discussions of "natural social bonds" and the medieval synthesis.

6. Given that history of abuse, some suggest that the community of faith today would be well advised to lay aside the military metaphor and to find other ways of portraying God's action. Here it suffices to observe that the prophets, later historians, and the New Testament both relativize and transform the royal image, as will be further shown in the fourth section.

7. This introduction is adapted and quoted from introductions written by Donald Durnbaugh to "War Is Contrary to the Will of God" and "Peace Is the Will of God" in Donald F. Durnbaugh, Ed., *On Earth Peace* (Elgin, Ill.: The Brethren Press, 1978), pp. 46, 73.

8. The quotations from the Oxford and Amsterdam Reports are annotated by the initials Ox and A and by page numbers taken from:

The Churches Survey Their Task, The Report of the Conference at Oxford, July 1937, "On Church, Community and State" (London, 1938).

The First Assembly of the World Council of Churches, Held at Amsterdam August 22 to September 4, 1948 (London, 1949).

9. The Church of the Brethren, the various kinds of Mennonites, and Quakers have been grouped as the "historic peace churches" ever since 1935.

10. This summary and chronology was prepared initially in response to the request of the Friends World Committee for Consultation (London) for use at an IFOR/HPC consultation at Assisi in August 1988. A few of the details have been traced by courtesy of the Mennonite Church Archives (Leonard Gross) at Goshen, Ind., but no careful archival search has been made. Corrections, or notification of research interests would be appreciated. Please send them to John Howard Yoder, 348 Decio Hall, Notre Dame, IN 46556.

11. On this history cf. John S. Conway, "The Struggle for Peace Between the Wars," *Ecumenical Review*, vol. 35, n.1 (January 1983):25-40.

12. Consisting of about 5,000 words, it was first printed in *Fellowship*, Fellowship of Reconciliation, September 1948, vol. XIV, no. 8, pp. 17-24.

13. Cited in Donald Durnbaugh, ed. *On Earth Peace* (Brethren Press: Elgin, Ill.) 1978, p. 40 (hereafter cited in the text as DB:pp).

14. Sources: letter of August 11, 1951, from M. R. Zigler and WCC Central Committee Minutes.

15. See also *Ecumenical Review*, vol. 25, no. 4 (Oct. 1973): 434-446.

The Authors

Douglas Gwyn teaches at Pendle Hill (Wallingford, Pa.). He holds an M.Div. and S.T.M. from Union Theological Seminary (New York) and a Ph.D. from Drew University. His published works include *Apocalypse of the Word: The Life and Message of George Fox* (Richmond, Ind.: Friends United Press, 1986) and numerous articles in *Quaker Religious Thought*.

George Hunsinger is associate professor of Theology at Bangor Theological Seminary (Maine). He holds an M.A., M.Phil., and Ph.D. from Yale University. His broad experience as a lecturer includes presenting, in Geneva, Switzerland, "The Church's Mission in the Nuclear Age," a paper commissioned by the World Alliance of Reformed Churches.

Eugene F. Roop is Wieand professor of Biblical Studies at Bethany Theological Seminary (Chicago). He holds an M.Div. from Bethany Theological Seminary and a Ph.D. from Claremont Graduate School. He is a widely traveled lecturer and author of numerous articles and books, including the forthcoming *Heard in Our Land* (Brethren Press).

John Howard Yoder is professor of Theology at the University of Notre Dame (Ind.). He holds a Th.D. from the University of Basel (Switzerland). His publications and teaching range over the fields of reformation history, church renewal, biblical interpretation, ecumenism and missiology, and Christian ethics. His best-known book is *The Politics of Jesus* (Eerdmans, 1972).